T0286772

Cambridge Elements ⁼

Elements in the Renaissance
edited by
John Henderson
Birkbeck, University of London, and Wolfson College, University of Cambridge
Jonathan K. Nelson
Syracuse University Florence

ELITE WOMEN AND THE ITALIAN WARS, 1494–1559

Susan Broomhall
Australian Catholic University

Carolyn James
Monash University

CAMBRIDGE
UNIVERSITY PRESS

Shaftesbury Road, Cambridge CB2 8EA, United Kingdom

One Liberty Plaza, 20th Floor, New York, NY 10006, USA

477 Williamstown Road, Port Melbourne, VIC 3207, Australia

314–321, 3rd Floor, Plot 3, Splendor Forum, Jasola District Centre,
New Delhi – 110025, India

103 Penang Road, #05–06/07, Visioncrest Commercial, Singapore 238467

Cambridge University Press is part of Cambridge University Press & Assessment,
a department of the University of Cambridge.

We share the University's mission to contribute to society through the pursuit of
education, learning and research at the highest international levels of excellence.

www.cambridge.org
Information on this title: www.cambridge.org/9781009462686

DOI: 10.1017/9781009415972

First published 2023

A catalogue record for this publication is available from the British Library

ISBN 978-1-009-46268-6 Hardback
ISBN 978-1-009-41595-8 Paperback
ISSN 2631-9101 (online)
ISSN 2631-9098 (print)

Elite Women and the Italian Wars, 1494–1559

Elements in the Renaissance

DOI: 10.1017/9781009415972
First published online: December 2023

Susan Broomhall
Australian Catholic University

Carolyn James
Monash University

Author for correspondence: Susan Broomhall, Susan.Broomhall@acu.edu.au

Abstract: This Element analyses the critical importance of elite women to the conflict conventionally known as the Italian Wars that engulfed much of Europe and the Mediterranean between 1494 and 1559. Through its considered attention to the interventions of women connected to imperial, royal, and princely dynasties, we show the breadth and depth of the opportunities, roles, impact, and influence that certain women had to shape the course of the conflict both in wartime activities and in peacemaking. The Element thus expands the ways in which we can think about women's participation in war and politics. It makes use of a wide range of sources such as literature, art, and material culture, as well as more conventional text forms. Women's voices and actions are prioritised in making sense of evidence and claims about their activities.

Keywords: early modern women, Italian Wars, gender, Habsburg, Valois

ISBNs: 9781009462686 (HB), 9781009415958 (PB), 9781009415972 (OC)
ISSNs: 2631-9101 (online), 2631-9098 (print)

Contents

Introduction

The Italian Wars, also known as the Habsburg–Valois Wars, were a series of fractured military clashes interspersed with moments of peace which began in 1494 and continued for some six decades. It was the most significant and defining conflict in Europe during the late medieval to early modern period. While the fighting was mostly concentrated geographically in Italy, the ramifications of the Wars were felt across Europe. By the signing of the Treaty of Cateau-Cambrésis in April 1559, much of the continent had been drawn into the Wars' organised violence, since not only France, Spain, the Holy Roman Empire, and many Italian states had become embroiled in the conflagration, so too had England, Scotland, and the Ottoman Empire.

When the French king Charles VIII set off over the Alps with a large army to claim the kingdom of Naples in 1494, the far-reaching consequences of his actions were little imaginable. Charles insisted that the southern Italian realm belonged to him through inheritance from the Angevin dynasty, which had ruled the kingdom until 1442, when it had fallen to the crown of Aragon. The French occupation of Naples in early 1495 following the abject failure of the Aragonese monarch to defend his regime took Italian and European rulers by surprise. Indeed, Charles VIII's dramatic success sparked widespread alarm and was the catalyst for a series of relatives and interested parties, including Ferdinand (Ferdinand II of Aragon, Ferdinand V of Castile) and Maximilian I of Austria, to respond by helping to restore the Aragonese to power and to chase the French from the Italian peninsula. Charles' death in 1498 seemed to close this chapter of European conflict. Milan, however, soon emerged as a new flashpoint. Charles' successor, Louis XII, claimed title to the wealthy duchy by right of descent from his grandmother Valentina Visconti. Once again, competing claims entangled rulers of state and church in military engagements reflecting complex alliances and rivalries, positions that were inherited and violently pursued by successive generations of the conflict's leading dynasties.[1] The Wars may have started over territorial control of Naples, but they spiralled out to encompass the engagement of lands and people in wider Europe, the Near East, and North Africa, and as far away as the Spanish colonies in central and south America, where some veterans of the conflict turned conquistadors. The resources of the Americas supplied considerable economic firepower that sustained Habsburg involvement in the Wars.[2]

---

[1] On the harrowing social and political consequences within Milan of the nine changes of government in just thirty years during the Wars, see J. Gagné, *Milan Undone: Contested Sovereignties in the Italian Wars* (Cambridge, MA: Harvard University Press, 2021).

[2] On the significance of the riches coming from the Americas, see G. Parker, *Emperor: A New Life of Charles V* (New Haven, CT: Yale University Press, 2019), pp. 342–75. On the fiscal operations and precariousness of the Habsburg position, see also J. D. Tracy, *Emperor Charles V, Impresario*

The cultural impact of the encounters between the inhabitants of Italy's wealthy city states and the armies from beyond the Alps was a central feature of the epic histories of Jules Michelet and Jacob Burckhardt, who emphasised the role of the Wars in spreading the influence of Italian innovations in art, literature, and culture across Europe.[3] Their nineteenth-century visions of the gestation and export of the Renaissance from Italy to the rest of the continent are now mostly debunked, but there is still much to admire in these scholars' emphasis on social and cultural as well as political change, something often lacking in studies of the Italian Wars ever since. Even in quite recent literature, the conflicts are almost entirely discussed and presented from a politico-military perspective as a series of events in which statecraft, battle strategies, and new styles of combat combined to determine victory or defeat, and as political and diplomatic scenarios in which only men figure as protagonists.[4]

While there has been some consideration of how changing hierarchies of power within early modern Europe challenged traditional versions of masculinity and femininity, only a few studies have focused on the Italian Wars from this perspective.[5] A world in which a small number of remarkable women ruled, and in which many men were courtiers with negligible personal autonomy, created at least temporary instability in allocations of authority and work along strictly gendered lines. We investigate this phenomenon by examining the still little understood cultural behaviours and political contributions of the female members of the dynasties involved in the Wars. We examine too the significance of inter-dynastic family networks in determining or undermining alliances. By taking account of the insights provided by fifty years of gender research about the early modern period, which have stimulated new questions, theories, methods, and

---

of War: Campaign Strategy, International Finance, and Domestic Politics (Cambridge: Cambridge University Press, 2002).

[3] J. Michelet, *Histoire de France au seizième siècle* (Paris: Chamerot, 1855); J. Burckhardt, *Die Kultur der Renaissance in Italien* (Vienna: Phaidon, 1860).

[4] C. Shaw and M. Mallet, *The Italian Wars 1494–1559: War, State and Society in Early Modern Europe* (London: Routledge, 2014); M. Pellegrini, *Le guerre d'Italia 1494–1530* (Bologna: il Mulino, 2009); C. Shaw (ed.), *Italy and the European Powers: The Impact of War* (Leiden: Brill, 2006); A. Konstam, *Pavia 1525: The Climax of the Italian Wars* (Oxford: Osprey, 1996); D. Abulafia, *The French Descent into Italy, 1494–5: Antecedents and Effects* (Aldershot: Ashgate, 1995); F. L. Taylor, *The Art of War in Italy, 1494–1529* (Cambridge: Cambridge University Press, 1921).

[5] J. Najemy, 'Arms and letters: The crisis of courtly culture in the wars of Italy', in Shaw (ed.), *Italy and the European Powers*, pp. 207–38; J. Tylus, and G. Milligan (eds.), *The Poetics of Masculinity in Early Modern Italy and Spain* (Toronto: Toronto University Press, 2010); K. Long (ed.), *High Anxiety: Masculinity in Crisis in Early Modern France* (Kirksville, MO: Truman State University Press, 2002); L. Mansfield, *Representations of Renaissance Monarchy: Francis I and the Image-Makers* (Manchester: Manchester University Press, 2016); and L. Mansfield, 'The art of conjugal discord: A satirical double portrait of Francis I and Eleanor of Austria, c. 1530–1535', in P. Sherlock and M. Cassidy-Welch (eds.), *Practices of Gender in Late Medieval and Early Modern Europe* (Turnhout: Brepols, 2008), pp. 117–35.

sources for analysis, our goal is to investigate how dynastic, patrimonial, and familial structures of power, combined with the political, military, and social crises associated with the Italian Wars, required elite women's involvement in managing power during this time.

Gender Ideologies and the Italian Wars

Women as well as men were critical to the practice of war and both sexes were subject to contemporary gender ideologies that shaped military conduct and communication. Ideas about appropriate roles and distinct behaviours of women and men were asserted and reinforced, not only in prescriptive texts, but also in real life through overt performances of dominance and submission. Victory and defeat were proclaimed and understood in sexualised terms that spoke to assumptions about normative masculinities and femininities performed in heterosexual relations. Few people in Italy escaped the impact of decades of war in which opposing armies battled each other with new, more lethal weapons and innovative tactics, but still relied on terror to subdue towns and cities in their path.[6] Citizen diaries and chronicles document the ritual humiliations and sometimes vicious reprisals imposed on civilian populations by battle-hardened soldiers. The atrocities of the twenty-two-day Sack of Prato in 1512, for example, shocked the sensibilities even of those accustomed to the brutality of war. Prato, a small subject city within the Tuscan territorial state, was overrun by Spanish troops, under the command of Ramón Folc de Cardona, on their way to restore the Medici to a ruling position within nearby Florence. Eyewitness Jacopo Modesti recorded in his account of the sack that neither age, sex, nor status of any kind offered protection from the worst depredations of Spanish soldiers, which included unbridled sexual violence:

> [I]n sum, the sack was a universal despoliation of all things, people, and places, both sacred and profane. The rapes and incidences of incest and adultery, I do not want to mention out of shame: it is enough [to say] that they did not spare anyone, imprisoning noble women and girls who they happened upon and sparing neither the male or female sex, nor holy nuns, sodomizing them all brutally.[7]

Here we see an example of how the bodies of women and children, as well as those of conquered men, were used and perceived as sites on which other men's

---

[6] On the novel aspects of the Italian Wars, see M. Mallett, 'The transformation of war, 1494–1530', in Shaw (ed.), *Italy and the European Powers*, pp. 3–21.

[7] I. Modesti, 'Il miserando sacco dato alla terra di Prato dagli Spagnoli l'anno 1512', *Archivio storico italiano*, 1 (1842), 233–51 (242). For other contemporary accounts, see C. Guasti, *Scritti storici* (Prato: Stefano-Belli, 1894). All translations are our own unless otherwise stated. On complexities in contemporary responses to atrocities like the sack of Prato, see S. D. Bowd, *Renaissance Mass Murder: Civilians and Soldiers during the Italian Wars* (Oxford: Oxford University Press, 2018), pp. 173–92.

military control and conquest played out as deliberate acts of war, entrenching ideas about subordination as the behaviour of women or of men who had been rendered like women.

The physical and psychological harm that was directed against non-combatants by mercenary armies during the Italian Wars was certainly nothing new in the history of European warfare.[8] However, the printing revolution ensured that news of battles, sieges, and sacks of urban centres circulated widely, knowledge of the ubiquity of wartime rape provoking a painful awareness within Italy of the private and public dishonour associated with such attacks. The crisis of confidence in Italy's political systems and urban infrastructure provoked by the vulnerability of its towns and cities was expressed not only in sophisticated political critiques by intellectuals, but also in popularly consumed and mostly anonymous poems that explicitly characterised Italian cities assailed by war in feminised terms.[9] In a lengthy and vivid poem, the Venetian writer and satirist Pietro Aretino depicted the 1527 Sack of Rome as a brutal rape on 'the Pillar and sole Mistress of this great world, violated, begging on her knees, covered in blood, pitiable and weeping for herself'.[10]

A lost painting attributed to the Venetian artist Giorgione and usually referred to as *The Assault* is a rare visual representation of the same preoccupation with wartime rape as a measure of Italian powerlessness against foreign invasion (Figure 1). Known only through later copies, including this etching by the Flemish printmaker Quirin (Coryl) Boel, it depicts a soldier in early sixteenth-century military dress pressing his knee firmly against a nearly naked woman and threatening her with a dagger while dragging off her remaining item of clothing. It likely held broader metaphorical significance than the representation of a particular incident of sexual assault. The severed tree stump, brooding dark sky, and abandoned townscape, bristling with phallic towers, form the background to the hapless woman, alone in the countryside, but within sight of the town walls which had proved futile to keep her safe.[11]

Such explicitly sexualised representations of military valour as male dominance were a vital platform of political communication in the Wars. As Sarah A. Bendall has explored, the ceremonial armour of the military elite frequently visualised

[8] P. Bokody, 'Images of wartime sexual violence in the chronicles of Giovanni Villani and Giovanni Sercambi', *Renaissance Studies*, 36.4 (2021), 565–89.

[9] M. Beer, D. Diamanti, and C. Ivaldi (eds.), *Guerre in ottava rima*, 4 vols. (Modena: Edizioni Panini, 1989), vol. II: 'Guerre d'Italia (1483–1527)', pp. 857–64.

[10] D. Romei (ed.), *Scritti di Pietro Aretino nel codice Marciano IT.XI 66 (=6730)* (Florence: F. Cesati, 1987).

[11] See P. H. D. Kaplan, 'Giorgione's assault: War and rape in Renaissance Venice', in C. Baskins and L. Rosenthal (eds.), *Early Modern Visual Allegory: Embodying Meaning* (Aldershot: Ashgate, 2007), pp. 77–90.

Figure 1 Quirin Boel (printmaker), after Giorgione, *Woman and a Soldier in a Landscape*, 1660; engraving/etching on paper, 176 mm x 242 mm, David Teniers (II) (publisher). Rijksmuseum, Amsterdam, RP-P-2014-60-25

classically inspired tropes and feminised allegories to convey messages about the wearer's political superiority and successful subordination of enemies.[12] For example, a 1537 portrait medal of François I of France depicts him in profile wearing the laurel wreath of a Roman emperor and holding a staff with a fleur-de-lis. The reverse of the medallion shows a male figure in armour on horseback, arm raised with sword in hand, trampling the naked female figure of Fortuna. The inscription reads 'DE VICIT FORTVNAM VIRTVTE' ('He has vanquished fortune through virtue') (Figure 2). The medallion was probably struck to celebrate the French victories in northern Italy the year before. Here the masculine *virtù* in warfare defeats the feminine Fortuna. Niccolò Macchiavelli's *The Prince*, written around 1513 in the aftermath of the defeat of the Florentine republic by a Spanish-backed Medicean regime, depicted Fortuna as a forceful and unruly woman who had to be beaten and coerced into submission by a virile man: 'being a woman, she favours young men, because they are less circumspect and more ardent, and because they command her with greater audacity'.[13] Thus, according to this view of male

---

[12] S. A. Bendall, 'Female personifications and masculine forms: Gender, armour and allegory in the Habsburg–Valois conflicts of sixteenth-century Europe', *Gender & History*, 35.1 (2023), 42–67.

[13] N. Macchiavelli, *The Prince*, trans. G. Bull (London: Penguin Books, 2004), p. 108. See H. F. Pitkin, *Fortune Is a Woman: Gender and Politics in the Thought of Niccolò Machiavelli* (Berkeley: California University Press, 1984), pp. 139–69.

Figure 2 Benvenuto Cellini, medallion of François I, reverse showing Virtue
conquering Fortune, cast *c*.1537, electrotype medal replica. Heath Warwick
(photographer), Museums Victoria, Number 2014243

agency, if a prince could take control of Fortuna's metaphorical rudder and
turn the tide of a battle, the power of men was reinforced, not challenged, by
her presence.

Gendered choreography and language also featured in intricately orches-
trated military rituals such as the triumphal entry of victorious armies into
defeated towns and cities. Noblewomen were expected to look on from balcon-
ies and windows at male martial performances that required affirmation through
the female gaze, while women of lower status were ordered by authorities to line
the streets as a symbol of their community's subordination and vulnerability.[14]
Elizabeth Reid's recent study of the entries of French armies into Genoa high-
lights the ways in which gendered performance and allegory were intrinsic to
the negotiation and articulation of political relationships.[15] Moreover, lower-status
women were often perceived by the male protagonists of the Wars as sexual objects
available for exchange in the making of male relationships and alliances, as John
Gagné has shown.[16]

Ready access to a succession of women's bodies was rendered an essential
aspect of everyday soldiering. Elite men such the military captain, Giovanni de'

---

[14] A. Dialeti, 'Defending women, negotiating masculinity in early modern Italy', *Historical
Journal*, 54.1 (2011), 1–23; G. Milligan, *Moral Combat: Women, Gender, and War in Italian
Renaissance Literature* (Toronto: University of Toronto Press, 2018), pp. 154–6.

[15] E. Reid, 'Gendering political relationships in Genoese ceremonial entries', *Sixteenth Century
Journal*, 52.1 (2021), 79–110; see also E. Reid, 'Female representation and violence in the
ceremonial entries of the Italian Wars', *Renaissance Studies*, 36.5 (2022), 750–68.

[16] J. Gagné, 'Collecting women: Three French kings and manuscripts of empire in the Italian
Wars', *I Tatti Studies in the Italian Renaissance*, 20.1 (2017), 127–84.

Medici, known as Giovanni delle Bande Nere, included the provision of prostitutes in letters ordering essential war supplies from his treasurer and lieutenant, Francesco Albizi. Giovanni's correspondence mentions sex workers from all over the peninsula, including Flora from Padua, Angelica from Venice, Nicolosa 'the painted Jewess', and a Greek slave called Lorenzina.[17] Other commanders, including Francesco Gonzaga, the marquis of Mantua, behaved in the same fashion. While encamped outside Bologna in the autumn of 1506, during Pope Julius II's siege of the city, Francesco accepted a young boy as his bedfellow after his courtiers failed to secure a prostitute for their master due to the high demand from other elite soldiers.[18] Michael Rocke's scholarship on male sexuality has focused on Renaissance Florence, but his insights are applicable in other contemporary contexts. While Francesco's sexual encounter with a youth would have been technically sinful if it included sodomy, as the dominant and active partner, the marquis could display his sexual virility just as effectively with a boy as with a woman.[19] That he associated his own sexual potency with military success is suggested by the fact that he closed up a letter to his secretary, which proclaimed the reclaiming of Genoa by the French king Louis XII, with a pornographic seal based on an ancient Roman brothel token.[20]

Women's Activities during the Wars

The Italian Wars, we argue, were thus made in and through contemporary gender ideologies. However, this did not mean women only experienced the conflict as (real or symbolic) victims of male violence. Historians have long recognised that military conflicts sometimes provided new tools and opportunities for women across the social spectrum.[21] The Italian Wars were no exception, even if we must work hard to glimpse the activities of non-elite women behind the political and military scenes. One of the most significant and lavish diplomatic events

---

[17] A. Fornaciari, R. Gaeta, S. Minozzi, and V. Giuffra, 'Syphilis in Maria Salviati (1499–1543), wife of Giovanni de' Medici of the Black Bands', *Emerging Infectious Diseases*, 26.6 (2020), 1274–82 (1280).

[18] A. Luzio, 'Isabella d'Este di fronte a Giulio II negli ultimi tre anni del suo pontificato', *Archivio storico lombardo*, 17 (1912), 245–334, and 18 (1912), 55–144, and 393–456 (vol. 17, p. 254).

[19] M. Rocke, *Forbidden Friendships, Homosexuality and Male Culture in Renaissance Florence* (Oxford: Oxford University Press, 1996).

[20] M. Bourne, 'Mail humour and male sociability: Sexual innuendo in the epistolary domain of Francesco II Gonzaga', in S. F. Matthews-Grieco (ed.), *Erotic Cultures of Renaissance Italy* (Aldershot: Ashgate, 2010), pp. 199–221 (p. 205).

[21] See, for example, the analysis of the English Civil War on women's publication in P. Crawford, 'Women's published writings 1600–1700', in M. Prior (ed.), *Women in English Society, 1500–1800* (London: Routledge, 1985), pp. 211–31.

associated with the Wars involved a huge amount of expert female labour. The extant records for the Field of Cloth of Gold provide clues about the production by female craft workers of the highly refined artefacts that were on display during the magnificently staged meeting between Henry VIII and François I at Calais in 1520. More women than men were employed in making the tapestries for the estimated 300 to 400 richly decorated tents prepared for the occasion.[22]

Women also operated in under-recognised roles as what has recently been termed 'shadow agents of war'.[23] In a volume devoted to the labour that non-combatants performed to support and sustain armies, edited by Stephen Bowd, Sarah Cockram, and John Gagné, women and children are shown to be important members of the military community. They worked in camp laundries, scrounged for food, prepared meals, and even took part in sieges and sacks. At diplomatic meetings and military progresses, washerwomen travelled alongside the attendees and soldiers or provided their service to residents in nearby towns. The Swiss artist Niklaus Manuel Deutsch participated as a mercenary on French campaigns in the War of the League of Cambrai, serving as secretary to Albrecht von Stein, and later fought at Novara and in the Battle of Bicocca in 1522. He depicted female figures cooking and laundering within the camp.[24] Women and children who followed the troops moving across the continent also featured in contemporary prints, including in those produced by the Nuremberg printmaker Virgilius Solis, who depicted a female sutler, or canteen woman, in a series otherwise featuring male military figures (Figure 3).

While the work of ordinary women in supporting the everyday functioning of armies and of female artisans in supplying the magnificent accoutrements of warrior kings is beginning to emerge, building on such research is beyond the scope of this Element. Here we focus on how elite women engaged in the Wars and consider what agency might mean in this context. A woman's high-born status might mean that she was more tightly observed and constrained than those lower down the social ladder. Yet it also gave some socially elevated individuals the capacity to manoeuvre and certainly provided them with more opportunities than ordinary women to have their activities and thoughts documented. Scholarship on the lives of elite women in early modern Europe has revealed just how important

---

[22] Bibliothèque Nationale, Paris, MS fr. 10,383, fols. 39r–132r, cited in G. Richardson, *The Field of Cloth of Gold* (New Haven, CT: Yale University Press, 2013), p. 43.

[23] S. Bowd, S. Cockram, and J. Gagné (eds.), *Shadow Agents of Renaissance War: Suffering, Supporting, and Supplying Conflict in Italy and Beyond* (Amsterdam: Amsterdam University Press, 2023).

[24] See also C. Andersson, 'Harlots and camp followers: Swiss Renaissance drawings of young women circa 1520', in E. S. Cohen and M. Reeves (eds.), *The Youth of Early Modern Women* (Amsterdam: Amsterdam University Press, 2018), pp. 117–34.

Figure 3 Virgilius Solis (printmaker), *Female Sutler and Boy with a Dead Rooster*, from the series *Military Figures in Landscapes*, 1524–1562; engraving/etching on paper, 112 mm x 82 mm. Rijksmuseum, Amsterdam, RP-P-OB-54.785

they were as participants in the politics of dynasties across the European continent.[25] Recent studies also rethink how power was distributed within ruling houses, with Theresa Earenfight, for example, calling for analyses of rulership

---

[25] H. Hill (ed.), *Architecture and the Politics of Gender in Early Modern Europe* (Farnham: Ashgate, 2003); N. Akkerman and B. Houben (eds.), *The Politics of Female Households: Ladies-in-Waiting across Early Modern Europe* (Leiden: Brill, 2014); A. Cruz and M. Galli Stampino (eds.), *Early Modern Habsburg Women: Transnational Contexts, Cultural Conflicts, Dynastic Continuities* (London: Routledge, 2013); G. Sluga and C. James (eds.), *Women, Diplomacy and Politics since 1500* (London: Routledge, 2016); S. Broomhall and J. Van Gent, *Dynastic Colonialism: Gender, Materiality and the Early Modern House of Orange-Nassau* (London: Routledge, 2016); S. Broomhall and J. Van Gent, *Gender, Power and Identity in the Early Modern House of Orange-Nassau* (London: Routledge, 2016); A. Pearson (ed.), *Women and Portraits in Early Modern Europe: Gender, Agency, Identity* (London: Routledge, 2016); J. Daybell and S. Norrhem (eds.), *Gender and Political Culture in Early Modern Europe, 1400–1800* (London: Routledge, 2017); S. Broomhall (ed.), *Women and Power at the French Court, 1483–1563* (Amsterdam: Amsterdam University Press, 2018).

seen as 'a multiplicity of power relations'.[26] This is an important framework for more clearly elucidating the kinds of authority and influence that individuals were able to enact within contemporary structures of power and governance, especially in the atmosphere of crisis spawned by war. The particular gender dynamics of dynastic, patrimonial, and familial structures meant that women who were physically and emotionally close to Europe's male decision makers had the capacity to influence them, while others had more autonomous forms of authority. In exercising power, elite women usually worked *within* the contemporary gender ideologies that were repeatedly foregrounded in the Wars and theoretically restricted how they could contribute. In practice, however, the limitations (and the limited imagination that such assumptions about woman's capacity suggested) did not necessarily preclude significant levels of agency.

This Element aims to consider gender, as identity, ideology, and relations, as a lens through which to analyse the Italian Wars anew. However, it cannot be a comprehensive analysis of all the kinds of activities in which elite women were involved. We apply this theoretical approach as a guiding structure to three political contexts: those of the two major dynasties who were fomenting the conflict – the Habsburgs and the Valois – and that of Italian princely dynasties whose hold on power was threatened by the Wars. The sections to follow thus explore how varied political structures, and the different challenges that specific states faced in engaging with the Wars, shaped opportunities for elite women to be involved (and documented) in the conflicts' practices of power. Within these differing political contexts, we focus on individuals whose activities help us to demonstrate the range of roles open to elite women and to document the gendered constraints they faced, often eloquently articulated in their correspondence with male relatives. The lens of gender also guides the kinds of evidence we analyse. We pay particular attention to sources produced by women themselves and to the messages that they communicated, both directly and indirectly, in letters and literature, as well as through patronage of art and other cultural forms.

Sections 1 and 2 consider the political work of women in an empire and a kingdom, led by the dynastic houses of Habsburg and of Valois. In Section 1, we examine in particular the diverse activities of Mary of Hungary to support her brothers and her own diplomatic and financial initiatives in varied theatres of war. Section 2 analyses women of the French court, focusing on the diplomacy and intellectual outreach of Marguerite de Navarre, as well as her engagement with

---

[26] T. Earenfight, 'Without the persona of the prince: Kings, queens, and the idea of monarchy in late medieval Europe', *Gender & History* 19.1 (2007), 1–21 (esp. pp. 11–15); L. Geevers and M. Marini (eds.), *Dynastic Identity in Early Modern Europe: Rulers, Aristocrats and the Formation of Identities* (London: Routledge, 2016); E. Woodacre, L. H. S. Dean, C. Jones, Z. E. Rohr, and R. E. Martin (eds.), *The Routledge History of Monarchy*, 4 vols. (London: Routledge, 2019).

the Wars' cultural, religious, and sexual politics in her literary work, the *Heptaméron*. In Section 3, we turn to the complicated power structures of the Italian peninsula, and the dynastic houses that governed Italy's northern principalities specifically, to consider the political work of women such as Isabella d'Este, the diplomacy from France of her sister-in-law, Clara Gonzaga, and the survival strategies of Lucrezia Borgia that shored up the Este regime in Ferrara.

Isabella d'Este and Marguerite de Navarre have been well studied as leading, even unique figures within the cultural scene of their day. Here, we provide a new perspective about these individuals by analysing them with reference to other similarly well-educated and politically literate women in a range of dynastic contexts. Collectively, our analysis demonstrates just how profoundly the course of the Italian Wars depended upon elite women's participation in diplomacy and their contributions to the logistics of warfare. We show that contemporary gender ideology certainly complicated women's involvement. However, in showcasing their administrative competence and diplomatic talents, women demonstrated that the ongoing philosophical defences of the female sex that were advanced in the long-running, contemporary intellectual debate known as the *querelle des femmes* could have real-world application.

1 Managing War: Women in the Habsburg Dynastic Business

In this section, we examine how the distributed Habsburg empire created opportunities for women to make crucial financial, diplomatic, and aesthetic contributions to the dynasty's wartime activities. We explore how the patriarch enlisted the service of female relatives through affective rhetoric which aimed to compel action expected to flow from certain relationships and which was critical to an individual's status within the family. We demonstrate that in sites as diverse as letters, art, and clothing, women used this same language of family and feelings to assert agency and identities for themselves in the contexts of war and peace that the Italian Wars created.

We take as our particular focus Mary of Hungary.[27] She is well known to scholars as one of the most influential women of the period through her long tenure of almost twenty-five years as regent of the Netherlands on behalf of her older brother, Charles V. Scholars have explored her court life, her engagement

---

[27] The individuals analysed in this Element are named in contemporary sources and modern scholarship in various ways. Here, we are guided by the important structural and conceptual contexts in which women were operating. In Section 1, the names of the Habsburg women emphasise the vast extent of the empire that their work supported, while those in Sections 2 and 3 foreground the culturally and physically unified locales of the courts in which French and Italian noblewomen participated.

with music, and her possible interest in Lutheran beliefs.[28] Her correspondence with Charles documents the challenging duties not only of controlling foment in the region, but of communicating effectively with her brother.[29] However, in an earlier period, Mary also played a perhaps more pivotal political role in relation to the wider trajectory of the Italian Wars, during the decade in which she resided in the kingdom of Hungary, as wife and then widow of Lajos II, from 1521 to 1531. Mary was instrumental to the Habsburg dynasty's ability to retain control over a sizeable portion of the kingdom. Her political skills ensured that her brothers, the Holy Roman Emperor Charles V and Ferdinand, Archduke of Austria and King of Bohemia and Habsburg Hungary, continued to access vital support for their military campaigns across Europe from the fertile lands of Hungary. Mary's activities to secure Ferdinand's authority in the region, however, also helped to solidify the collaboration of Habsburg enemies, most notably the Ottoman sultan, Suleiman I, and the French king, François I.[30] They partnered with Ferdinand's local rival for power, Zápolya János, developing an important set of relations that shaped diplomacy and warfare for the rest of the Wars. Mary's correspondence with Ferdinand during this period and afterwards forms a key source for understanding her activities. In these letters, we see the development of her style of interaction with Ferdinand that, in both its successes and its failures, would become crucial to the events that shaped the latter half of the Wars.

Pompeo Leoni's bronze figures prepared for the tomb of Charles V, depicted here in Juan Pantoja de la Cruz's 1599 painting, presented a powerful version of how male dynasts expected Habsburg power to operate. Charles is depicted kneeling next to his wife, Isabel of Portugal, with his sisters Eleanor and Mary

---

[28] O. Réthelyi, B. F. Romhányi, E. Spekner, and A. Végh (eds.), *Mary of Hungary: The Queen and Her Court 1521–1531*, trans. A. Harmath, B. F. Romhányi, and G. Trostovszky (Budapest: Budapest History Museum, 2005–6); M. Fuchs and O. Réthelyi (eds.), *Maria von Ungarn (1505–1558): Eine Renaissancefürstin* (Muenster: Achendorff, 2007); B. Federinov and G. Docquier (eds.), *Marie de Hongrie: Politique et culture sous la renaissance aux Pays-Bas. Actes du Colloque tenu au Musée royal de Mariemont les 11 et 12 novembre 2005* (Mariemont: Collections monographies du Musée royal de Mariemont, 2008); N. G. Perez (ed.), *Mary of Hungary, Renaissance Patron and Collector: Gender, Art and Culture* (Turnhout: Brepols, 2020).

[29] L. V. G. Gorter-van Royen and J.-P. Hoyois (eds.), *Correspondance de Marie de Hongrie avec Charles Quint et Nicolas de Granvelle*, 2 vols. (Turnhout: Brepols, 2009–18), vol. I (2009): '1532 et années antérieures'. On her role as regent of the Netherlands, see J. de Iongh, *Mary of Hungary: Second Regent of the Netherlands*, trans. M. D. Herter Norton (New York: W. W. Norton, 1958); L. V. G. Gorter-van Royen, *Maria von Hongarije, regentes der Nederlanden: Een politieke analyse op basis van haar regentschapsordonnaties en haar corespondentie met Karel V* (Leiden: Hilversum, 1995); and D. R. Doyle, 'The sinews of Habsburg governance in the sixteenth century: Mary of Hungary and political patronage', *Sixteenth Century Journal*, 31.2 (2000), 349–60.

[30] C. Isom-Verhaaren, *Allies with the Infidel: The Ottoman and French Alliance in the Sixteenth Century* (London: Bloomsbury, 2013); P. Barthe, *French Encounters with the Ottomans, 1510–1560* (London: Routledge, 2016); S. Broomhall, 'Alter egos: Mediterranean agents negotiating identity at the dawn of the Franco-Ottoman alliance', in Z. E. Rohr and J. W. Spangler (eds.), *Significant Others: Aspects of Deviance and Difference in Premodern Europe* (London: Routledge, 2021), pp. 81–109.

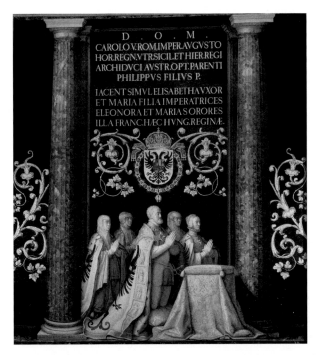

D . O . M .
CAROLO V.ROM.IMPER.AVGVSTO
HOR.REGN.VTR.SICIL.ET HIER.REGI
ARCHIDVCI AVSTR.OPT.PARENTI
PHILIPPVS FILIVS P.

IACENT SIM VL ELISABETHA VXOR
ET MARIA FILIA IMPERATRICES
ELEONORA ET MARIA S ORORES
ILLA FRANC.HÆC HVNG.REGINÆ.

Figure 4 Juan Pantoja de la Cruz, *The sculpted bronze figures produced by Pompeo Leoni of Charles V, Isabel of Portugal, Eleanor of Austria, Mary of Hungary, Maria of Austria*, oil on canvas, 1599; San Lorenzo del Escorial, Madrid. Alamy

behind him, accompanied by his daughter Maria (Figure 4). Dynastic structures of power organisation and operation distributed positions of governance among family members, who were assumed to share motivation and commitment to objectives typically determined by its leading man.[31] In 1543, Charles wrote a holograph document for his son, Philip, advising him how to rule. He weighed up the attributes of his various ministers and the factionalism that charged disputes between them.[32] He did not present a similar analysis of his relatives; ministers were potentially disposable, but family members remained at Charles' beck and call, their own ambitions and desires often ignored where they clashed with his vision of Habsburg governance.

Induction into the dynastic duties of individuals was an important task that fell into the training repertoire of elder Habsburg women such as Margaret of Austria who assumed a significant role in orienting Charles to his duties and inculcating

---

[31] For comparative analysis of gender and power structures within a competing dynasty, see the discussion of gendered power structures in an early modern dynasty in Broomhall and Van Gent, *Gender, Power and Identity.*

[32] Parker, *Emperor*, p. 58.

filial loyalty to him in his siblings.[33] Charles appeared to embrace the job that he was to perform. At their grandfather's death in 1516, the fifteen-year-old insisted to his younger brother Ferdinand that 'in us you have gained your only brother, but also (as you will see) a true father'.[34] A reading of the letters from the siblings to Charles suggests that they too had learned how to perform their dynastic role. Thus, when, in 1519, Charles opposed Ferdinand being put forward as a compromise candidate to be the King of the Romans, Ferdinand outwardly expressed acceptance: 'I place my entire fate in your hands, as in the hands of my lord and father, because that is how I see you and will see you for my whole life.'[35] Younger sisters Catherine and Mary referred to Charles respectively as 'the common father to us all' and as the central figure in their lives: 'after God, Your Majesty means everything to me'.[36] Even his elder sister, Eleanor, assured her brother: 'I have never wanted to take a decision without knowing the pleasure of Your Majesty, whom I regard as my sovereign and my father.'[37] The edges of political performance and lived feelings are difficult to discern, although such expressions continued to be articulated to Charles even after his abdication.

The demands upon the dynasties' leading men to be physically present in a wide range of geographically dispersed political and military events during the Italian Wars, precisely because they were the recognised face of authority, drew a far wider network of kin into roles of governance and distributed power more broadly than ever before. Charles' close relatives were vital agents in the control of the geographically vast and culturally distinct regions that made up the Habsburg empire.[38] As Archduke of Austria from 1521, younger brother

[33] A. J. Gschwend, '*Ma meilleur soeur*: Leonor of Austria, queen of Portugal and France', in F. Checa Cremades (ed.), *Los Inventarios de Carlos V y la Familia Imperial*, 3 vols. (Madrid: Fernando Villaverde, 2010), vol. III, pp. 2569–92.

[34] Charles to Ferdinand, 15 February 1516, in D. C. Spielman and C. Thomas, 'Quellen zur Jugend Erzherzog Ferdinands I. in Spanien: Bisher unbekannte Briefe Karls V. an seinen Bruder (1514–1517)', *Mitteilungen des Österreichischen Staatsarchiv*, 37 (1984), 1–34 (21–2); translated in Parker, *Emperor*, p. 56.

[35] Ferdinand to Charles, February 1519, cited in R. Fagel, 'Don Fernando en Flandes (1518–1521): Un príncipe sin tierra', in A. Alvar and F. Edelmayer (eds.), *Fernando I, 1503–1564: Socialización, vida privada y actividad pública de un Emperador del renacimiento* (Madrid: Sociedad Estatal de Conmemoraciones Culturales, 2004), pp. 253–71 (p. 270); translated in Parker, *Emperor*, p. 217.

[36] Catherine to Charles, 31 January 1532, in A. Viaud (ed.), *Lettres des souverains portugais à Charles-Quint et à l'Impératrice (1528–1532)* (Lisbon: Centre Culturel Calouste Gulbenkian, 1994), p. 176; and Mary to Charles [End August 1555], in C. Weiss (ed.), *Papiers d'Etat du Cardinal de Granvelle*, 9 vols. (Paris: Imprimerie nationale, 1841–52), vol. IV (1843), p. 469; translated in Parker, *Emperor*, p. 219.

[37] Eleanor to Charles, November 1556, L. P. Gachard (ed.), *Retraite et mort de Charles-Quint au monastère de Yuste*, 3 vols. (Brussels: M. Hayez, 1854–5), vol. II (1855), p. 113; translated in Parker, *Emperor*, p. 219.

[38] For a recent study, see T. Ylä-Anttila, 'Habsburg female regents in the early sixteenth century', unpublished PhD thesis, University of Helsinki (2019).

Ferdinand acted as a mediator between Charles and the German and Austrian lands and princes. As King of Bohemia and Royal Hungary from 1526, and later Croatia, he shored up Habsburg control of the eastern territories. Beyond the patriarch of the dynasty, those with the most opportunity to forge their own path were younger men who were only temporarily subordinate and who, by right of patrilineage, could expect one day to become the dynasty's leader in their turn. Both Charles' brother, Ferdinand, and Charles' eldest son, Philip, occupied such positions. Charles had thus to juggle the promise of influence and succession between both, so that they remained motivated to follow his plan and not deviate from it in pursuit of their own interests. The political roles and ambitions of the Habsburg women did not need to be policed so intently. They remained subordinate, their power as regents temporary, even if, as in the case of Mary, it endured for decades. They were expected always to serve and promote the military ambitions and political agendas of the dynasty's leading men.

Diplomatic Bodies

Strategic marriages that united dynasties through ties of blood were key to Habsburg success.[39] In 1521, Mary, the sixth child of joint monarchs Joanna and Philip I of Castile (see Figure 5), raised under the care of her aunt, Margaret of Austria, arrived in Hungary to marry Lajos II, ensuring that her brothers would have vital dynastic and resource support for their military campaigns from the Jagiellons and their lands.

Mary followed a pattern reflected in the experiences of her sisters, each of whom was expected to make a prized alliance for the Habsburgs. For example, older sister Eleanor was no stranger to marriage that served the needs of her brother Charles.[40] The eldest of the six Habsburg siblings, she had first married in 1518 the twice-widowed Manuel of Portugal, formerly the husband of two of

---

[39] For analyses of marriage politics in the Habsburg dynasty, see P. S. Fichtner, 'Dynastic marriage in sixteenth-century Habsburg diplomacy and statecraft: An interdisciplinary approach', *American Historical Review*, 81.2 (1976), 243–65; J. F. Patrouch, '"Bella gerant alli". Laodamia's sisters, Habsburg brides: Leaving home for the sake of the house', in Cruz and Galli Stampino (eds.), *Early Modern Habsburg Women*, pp. 25–40; D. von Güttner-Sporzyński, 'Daughter, mother, widow: The making of the identities of Isabella d'Aragona', *Gender & History*, early view (2023), https://doi.org/10.1111/1468-0424.12683. On the marriage strategies of the previous generation of Habsburgs, see D. von Güttner-Sporzyński, 'Contextualising the marriage of Bona Sforza to Sigismund I of Poland: Maximilian I's diplomacy in Italy and Central Europe', *Folia Historica Cracoviensia*, 2 (2021), 69–90.

[40] For a biographical study of Eleanor's life, see G. de Boom, *Archiduchesse Éléonore, reine de France: Soeur de Charles Quint* (Brussels: Le Cri, 1943).

Figure 5 Jan van Nieu(landt) (printmaker), *Charles V, Ferdinand I, Isabella, Eleanor, Catherine and Mary on horseback*, 1521–6; print, paper, 266 mm x 378 mm. Rijksmuseum, Amsterdam, RP-P-1928-138

her aunts. The marriage made her queen consort of Portugal. The union was short-lived but produced her only surviving daughter, Maria of Portugal. Eleanor's second marriage, this time to Charles' great enemy, François I, widower of Claude de France, in 1530, came about as a direct outcome of the Treaty of Cambrai, known as the Ladies' Peace because of the central role Margaret of Austria and Louise de Savoie played in its negotiation.

The 1529 Treaty of Cambrai, negotiated by Margaret on behalf of her nephew Charles V, and by Louise de Savoie for her son François I, recognised women's unique position to intervene in diplomatic negotiation. Elite women regularly negotiated activities that represented multiple dynastic identities. Charles' authority for Margaret to advance negotiations on his behalf represented her 'as aunt and mother'.[41] These relationships gave women authority to intervene in a crisis. As Margaret told her nephew,

---

[41] E. de Quinsonas, *Matériaux pour server à l'histoire de Marguerite d'Autriche*, 3 vols. (Paris: Delaroque Frères, 1860), vol. III, p. 342. See also C. Fletcher, 'The Ladies' Peace revisited: Gender, counsel and diplomacy', in H. Matheson-Pollack, J. Paul, and C. Fletcher (eds.), *Queenship and Counsel in Early Modern Europe* (Basingstoke: Palgrave, 2018), pp. 111–33; J. Dumont, L. Fagnart, N. Le Roux, and P.-G. Girault (eds.), *Les Paix des Dames, 1529: Diplomatie, genre et symbolique du pouvoir à la Renaissance* (Tours: Presses universitaires François-Rabelais, 2021).

'Madame the Regent and I will use our arts to soften matters.'[42] Margaret and Louise claimed that elite men's honour would not allow Charles and François to turn aside the allies and friends to whom they had made prior commitments in order to forge an agreement between Habsburg and Valois. These alliances were personal to these male leaders and invested in their sense of self. Margaret herself insisted that she and Louise were ideal to undertake negotiations because they could make no such personal commitments. Moreover, Margaret constructed elite male pride as intractable, while elite women's honour could be subordinated and compromised for dynastic goals.[43] In the service of peace, Margaret and Louise and their diplomatic agents articulated ideas about women's expertise in counterbalancing multiple relationships in which they sustained potentially competing loyalties, making 'the Ladies' Peace' a continuation of a conventional political system that was oriented around male political power.

Even after marriage, Habsburg women were expected to retain loyalty to their natal dynasty. Margaret and Louise had made a show of reconciliation between the warring dynasties central to the peace they devised, with Eleanor's marriage to François I one of its elements, but Margaret advised in her correspondence to Eleanor that the new bride should employ emotional intelligence and affective labour to understand her new Valois family and serve as a benign influence in favour of Habsburg interests: 'she will achieve more by sweetness than by pushing them too hard'.[44] Eleanor's astute assessments of her husband and the politics of the French court would in time provide Charles with valuable, intimate insights on Valois negotiations and strategy.[45]

Advising Brothers

The Wars' military campaigns and demand for personal intervention by dynastic leaders represented an opportunity for women, as consorts and female relatives, to take on official political roles as regents on a temporary basis. At the Battle of

---

[42] 8 February 1530, Archives générales du Royaume, Papiers d'Etat et d'Audience, no 38, pp. 248–9, cited in G. de Boom (ed.), *Correspondance de Marguerite d'Autriche et de ses ambassadeurs à la cour de France concernant l'exécution du traité de Cambrai, 1529–1530* (Brussels: Maurice Lamertin, 1935), p. xix. See also A.-J.-G. Le Glay (ed.), *Négociations diplomatiques entre la France et l'Autriche durant les trente premières années du XVIe siècle*, 2 vols. (Paris: Imprimerie royale, 1845).

[43] See further S. Broomhall, 'Les émotions genrées dans le cadre de la ratification du traité de Cambrai', in Dumont, Fagnart, Le Roux, and Girault (eds.), *Les Paix des Dames, 1529*, pp. 203–18.

[44] Margaret of Austria to Jean de La Sauch, secretary of Charles V, 21 July 1530, in Boom (ed.), *Correspondance*, p. 131.

[45] R. J. Knecht, 'Eléonore d'Autriche (1498–1558)', in C. Michon (ed.), *Les Conseillers de François Ier* (Rennes: Presses universitaires de Rennes, 2011), pp. 401–14, https://books.open edition.org/pur/120045?lang=en; see also Parker, *Emperor*, pp. 250–1.

Mohács, fought on an unpromising marshy landscape on 29 August 1526, Hungarian forces had been greatly outnumbered by the Ottoman army. Among the devastation, Lajos fell from his horse and drowned in his heavy armour. Mary, waiting for news of Hungary's success at Buda, discovered instead that she was now a widow. As Suleiman pressed on to an evacuated Buda, Mary's last moments in the city were spent ensuring that as much as possible of the kingdom's wealth in royal and religious treasures was stored in chests and carried away on the river to safety. She wrote to Ferdinand, then in Vienna, to send troops to protect her and his own claim to the now-vacant thrones of Hungary and Bohemia. She advised Ferdinand to come quickly to Hungary to stamp his authority on the wavering elite. Ferdinand thanked Mary and encouraged her continued reports: 'give me your good advice and counsel, as to how I can accede to the kingdoms of Hungary and Bohemia'.[46] However, he chose to secure first the crown of Bohemia and spent much of 1526 there while continuing to express gratitude for Mary's efforts and perspectives from the ground.

Ferdinand appointed Mary as his regent against the practice of Hungarian law that required the position be filled by the current Palatine. In Ferdinand's absence, Mary continued to seek support for her brother among the Hungarian aristocracy and to prepare for what would soon become a military conflict between Habsburg forces and those of the local rival, Zápolya János, who had worked among the Hungarian elite to have himself crowned king in November as the Diet met at Székesfehérvár. Mary responded by arranging a gathering of remaining members of the Diet at Pozsony, where Ferdinand, in absentia, was elected (also) king of Hungary. Mary warned that many nobles would expect significant bribes in return for their continued loyalty to the Habsburg cause, especially where they were suffering from food shortages on their lands. 'You can at this moment do with a florin what afterwards you will not be able to do with many,' she astutely advised.[47] Her letters interspersed these blunt assessments of the political and economic situation with expressions of hesitation, apology, and self-doubt: 'begging you again to not take it badly if I am so bold as to write to you so frankly, God knows, Monsieur, I do not proceed bad-heartedly but it pains me that your affairs do not go well, as we would wish them to'.[48]

---

[46] 11 September [1526], in W. Bauer and R. Lacroix (eds.), *Die Korrespondenz Ferdinands I*, 4 vols. (Vienna: Adolf Holzhausen, 1912–38), vol. I (1912), p. 447. On the political machinations of this period, see G. Pálffy, 'New dynasty, new court, new political decision-making: A decisive era in Hungary – the decades following the Battle of Mohács 1526', in Réthelyi, Romhányi, Spekner, and Végh (eds.), *Mary of Hungary*, pp. 27–39.

[47] 9 February [1527], in Bauer and Lacroix (eds.), *Die Korrespondenz Ferdinands I*, vol. II, part 1, p. 17.

[48] 9 February [1527], in Bauer and Lacroix (eds.), *Die Korrespondenz Ferdinands I*, vol. II, part 1, p. 18.

In his absence and that of his monies, Ferdinand pressed Mary to keep using honeyed words to sustain Hungarian supporters of the Habsburgs: 'begging you to maintain them still with good words in all good hope as best you can'.[49] In the summer of 1527, Ferdinand finally arrived in Hungary himself, securing Buda for the Habsburgs, and his forces prevailed when the two armies met at the Battle of Tarcal on 27 September. In February 1528, Ferdinand, confident that he now held the kingdom securely, prepared to leave. He asked Mary to act once again as his regent, recognising his sister's talents: '[I]t seemed to me that I could find no one better and more suited than you, madame my good sister, seeing that I can trust in you, and also your understanding and reputation and the experience that you have in these matters and the respect and fear that people will have for you.'[50] Mary, employing a technique that became important in her communication with her brother, declined forcefully, with humility:

> I do not know how to thank you humbly enough for the honour that it has pleased you to do me, together with the trust that you have in me … God knows that there can be nothing in the world that would give me greater pleasure than to do you service … but Monsieur I do not feel suited as to my person to do you service, for these matters are affairs for a person older and wiser than me.[51]

Expressions of doubt about her abilities, combined with proposals to retire from her role as regent, would also form a core aspect of the style of negotiation that she employed later with her eldest brother, Charles, especially when she did not agree with his decisions.

The role Ferdinand desired for Mary in Hungary followed a common pattern within the dynasty. In his instructions to his son Philip, written in 1548, Charles opined that 'it is never a good thing for the transaction of business – nor can I ever accept – to allow women to be involved in government unless they are married'.[52] The emperor indeed relied on a range of married women within his family to govern in his stead. Holy Roman Emperor Maximilian I advised a young Charles that he could seek out his aunt (Maximilian's daughter) Margaret of Austria 'on all your greatest and most difficult affairs, and take

[49] 5 March 1527, in Bauer and Lacroix (eds.), *Die Korrespondenz Ferdinands I*, vol. II, part 1, p. 25.

[50] 7 February 1528, Bauer and Lacroix (eds.), *Die Korrespondenz Ferdinands I*, vol. II, part 1, p. 189.

[51] 9 February 1528, Bauer and Lacroix (eds.), *Die Korrespondenz Ferdinands I*, vol. II, part 1, p. 191.

[52] Charles to Philip, 9 April 1548, in M. Fernández Álvarez (ed.), *Corpus Documental de Carlos V*, 5 vols. (Salamanca: Ediciones Universidad de Salamanca, 1973–81), vol. II (1975), pp. 612–15; translated in Parker, *Emperor*, p. 414.

and follow her advice' because 'by nature and nurture she cares for our interests and honour, and also yours: indeed we consider the three of us to be one and the same, united by a single desire and affection'.[53] Already, eight years earlier, Margaret had negotiated on behalf of her dynasty with Julius II and Louis XII, producing the League of Cambrai that confronted the Republic of Venice in the war that followed. Her influence among the League was recognised by the Doge Leonardo Loredano when he instructed his ambassador to England in 1510 to conclude peace with a range of the opposing side, including:

> With Maximilian, Emperor elect, or with his delegates; and also to negotiate a confederacy with said Emperor, with Henry King of England, with Ferdinand the Catholic King of Aragon, and with the widow Lady Margaret, the Emperors [*sic*] daughter, or any of them, one or more, or with their delegates.[54]

However, upon his majority in 1515, Charles dismissed Margaret as governor of the Netherlands. He soon changed his mind, recalling her to the role, where she remained until her death in 1530.

In her continuing role as governor, Margaret used strategic artistic commissions to assert loyalty to her nephew Charles. Dagmar Eichberger and Lisa Beaven have analysed Margaret's portrait collection at her Burgundian court within the context of her political alliances. Eichberger has also explored Margaret's shrewd use of art patronage to bolster her own authority and to advance the broader interests of the Habsburg dynasty during her later governorship of the Habsburg Netherlands.[55] She was likely responsible for commissioning a series of enamelled gold hat badges that depicted her nephew Charles V.[56] Each showed him wearing

---

[53] Maximilian to Charles, 18 January 1516, in L. P. C. van den Bergh, *Correspondance de Marguerite d'Autriche, gouvernante des Pays-Bas, avec ses amis, sur les affaires des Pays-Bas de 1506–1528* (Leiden: S. et J. Luchtmans, 1845–7), vol. II (1847), pp. 133–6; translated in Parker, *Emperor*, p. 48.

[54] 'Venice: January 1510', in R. Brown is the only editor no need to add the et al. (eds.), *Calendar of State Papers relating to English Affairs in the Archives of Venice 1509–1519*, 38 vols. (London: Her Majesty's Stationery Office, 1864–1947), vol. II (1867): '1509–1519'. *British History Online*, www.british-history.ac.uk/cal-state-papers/venice/vol2/pp10-14.

[55] D. Eichberger and L. Beaven, 'Family members and political allies: The portrait collection of Margaret of Austria', *Art Bulletin*, 77.2 (1995), 225–48; D. Eichberger, 'Margaret of Austria's portrait collection: Female patronage in the light of dynastic ambitions and artistic quality', *Renaissance Studies*, 10.2 (1996), 259–79; D. Eichberger, 'The culture of gifts: A courtly phenomenon from a female perspective', in D. Eichberger (ed.), *Women of Distinction: Margaret of York and Margaret of Austria* (Turnhout: Brepols, 2005), pp. 286–95; D. MacDonald, 'Collecting a new world: The ethnographic collections of Margaret of Austria', *Sixteenth Century Journal*, 33.3 (2002), 649–63.

[56] S. A. Bendall, 'Adorning masculinities? The commissioning and wearing of hat badges during the Habsburg–Valois Italian Wars', *Sixteenth Century Journal*, 52.3 (2021), 539–70;

the ceremonial chain of the Order of the Golden Fleece, one with his devise 'PLVS VLTRA' and another inscription listing all his Spanish titles. The images of Charles appear to derive from portraits made of the king while at Margaret's court.[57] Yvonne Hackenbroch has suggested that Margaret may have produced these badges to celebrate Charles' election as the Holy Roman Emperor in 1519.[58] Bendall proposes that the likely date and place of the manufacture of these two gold hat badges at Malines in 1520 suggests that Margaret may have commissioned them to be worn by members of her own court, perhaps for Charles' triumphal entry into the city of Antwerp in September that year.[59]

Another alliance key to the Habsburg's wartime activities was made through Charles' own marriage. In June 1525, he explained to his brother Ferdinand a series of reasons why marriage to Isabel of Portugal would assist his rule, his military campaigns, and the Habsburg dynasty.

> In order to leave these kingdoms under good order and government, I see no other remedy than to marry the Infanta Donna Isabella of Portugal, since the Cortes of the said kingdoms have required me to propose myself for such an union; and that on his part the King of Portugal offers me a million of ducats, most of them to be paid at once, in order to assist in defraying the expenses of our said journey into Italy. Were this marriage to take place, I could leave the Government here in the person of the said Infanta, who should be provided with a good council; so that there would be no apparent cause to fear any new movement.[60]

Isabel of Portugal was appointed regent of Castile, or Castile and Aragon, while Charles was on campaign and attending to his other territories, in 1528, between 1529 and 1533, 1535–6, and again in 1537–9.[61] In July 1529, Charles left for Rome to be crowned Holy Roman Emperor, leaving as regent Isabel, a twenty-six-year-old mother of two, pregnant with the couple's third child.[62] He had

---

Y. Hackenbroch, *Enseignes: Renaissance Hat Jewels* (Florence: Studio per Edizioni Scelte, 1996).

[57] Hackenbroch, *Enseignes*, p. 222.

[58] Y. Hackenbroch, 'Some portraits of Charles V', *Metropolitan Museum of Art Bulletin*, 27.6 (1969), 323–32 (325).

[59] Bendall, 'Adorning masculinities?'

[60] W. Bradford (ed.), *Correspondence of the Emperor Charles V and His Ambassadors at the Courts of England and France from the Original Letters in the Imperial Family Archives at Vienna with a Connecting Narrative and Biographical Notes of the Emperor and of Some of the Most Distinguished Officers of His Army and Household together with the Emperor's Itinerary from 1519–1551* (London: R. Bentley, 1850), p. 136.

[61] P. Marzahl, 'Communication and control in the political system of Emperor Charles V: The first regency of Empress Isabella', in W. Blockman and N. Mout (eds.), *The World of Emperor Charles V* (Amsterdam: Royal Netherlands Academy of Arts and Sciences, 2004), pp. 83–96.

[62] From the time of her marriage in 1526, Isabella was queen consort of the Spanish kingdoms and of the Romans, and Lady of the Netherlands. She was the Holy Roman Empress from 24 February 1530. On Isabel's political role, see recent biographical studies by A. Alvar

compiled instructions for his wife providing the powers of her regency. These set out that she was to consult each Friday with the royal council, led by Archbishop Tavera, and to communicate regularly with Charles for his advice on actions.[63] However, Isabel's firm views disturbed the royal council, which petitioned Charles to advise Isabel to trust in Tavera's advice and counsel.[64] Isabel herself wrote to Charles of the poor behaviour towards her among the noblemen.[65] There was only one voice she was interested in heeding, that of Charles himself. Isabel expressed concerns about delay to actions because of the time taken to have communication to and from Charles and begged him to respond more quickly to her letters.[66]

Managing Wartime Finances

In Hungary, Mary's actions were not simply to report to Ferdinand, and by extension to Charles, her perception of support for the Habsburg claims and to network among the kingdom's leading aristocrats. Hungary represented an important region that provided essential economic resources and food supplies to the central European territories of the empire, which helped to support the military efforts of the Habsburgs across Europe. Mary worked hard to protect the kingdom's assets, her husband's heritage, and her own entitlement as his widow, sometimes in a struggle against her own brother. In the months after she had ordered Buda's riches crated onto the Danube, Mary spent considerable time establishing their fate. Indeed, she framed her interest dramatically as a self-sacrificing willingness to assist Ferdinand, writing to him: 'not only this silverware but also all that I have up to my chemise will be ready to send to you, seeing your need'.[67]

Ezquerra, *La Emperatriz* (Madrid: La Esfera de los Libros, 2012); M. Gonzaga, *Imperatriz Isabel de Portugal* (Lisbon: Bertrand Editora, 2012); A. Villacorta Baños-García, *La Emperatriz Isabel* (Madrid: Actas, 2009); C. Seco Serrano, *La Emperatriz Isabel* (Madrid: Real Academia de la Historia, 2006); M. I. Piqueras Villaldea, *Carlos V y la Emperatriz Isabel* (Madrid: Actas, 2000). On her time as regent specifically, see M. Rubio Aragonés, 'Isabel de Portugal (1503–1539)', *Reinas de España, Las Austrias: Siglos XV–XVIII. De Isabel la Cátolica a Marian de Neoburgo* (Madrid: Esfera de los Libros, 2015), pp. 65–108; I. Jiménez Zamora, 'La actuación política de la Emperatriz Isabel (1528–1538)', *Espacio, tiempo y forma*, Serie IV: Historia Moderna 29 (2016), 163–85.

[63] 'Instruccion de Carlos V a Isabel', in Fernández Álvarez (ed.), *Corpus Documental de Carlos V*, vol. I (1973), pp. 131–3.

[64] Jiménez Zamora, 'La actuación política de la Emperatriz Isabel', p. 165.

[65] Jiménez Zamora, 'La actuación política de la Emperatriz Isabel', p. 167.

[66] Jiménez Zamora, 'La actuación política de la Emperatriz Isabel', p. 168.

[67] 1 September 1527, in Bauer and Lecroix (eds.), *Die Korrespondenz Ferdinands I*, vol. II, part 1, p. 115. On Mary's actions to secure these assets, see R. Orsolya, '" . . . Maria regina . . . nuda venerat ad Hungarium . . . ": The queen's treasures', in Réthelyi, Romhányi, Spekner, and Végh (eds.), *Mary of Hungary*, pp. 121–7.

In fact, in October 1527, Ferdinand had ordered János Bornemissza, castellan of Buda and *ispán* of Pozsony, to write up a list of what was in the chests. He asked that the items be categorised into three groups, A, B, and C. All the items listed in A would eventually be sent to Vienna, where the jewels were removed and the works smelted down for the greater glory of the Habsburg dynasty. Today, the details of these artefacts are known to us through their assessment on the list and by the calculations of master minter in Vienna, Thomas Behaim, of the gold, silver, and precious jewels that they yielded.[68] Those ranked as B and C were to remain in the kingdom as the assets of either the Hungarian crown or of Mary personally. Mary strongly asserted her own perspective on how Ferdinand had approached these precious resources that she had ensured survived the arrival of Suleiman into Buda. Of the artefacts that remained in the chests that were returned to her as part of Lajos' heritage, she complained in a letter to Ferdinand in May 1528, 'there is much which is not silverware or gold, or, in some parts, very little'.[69] And she had still not forgotten the matter more than a decade later when she calculated that 'jewels, gems, gold and silver to the value of six thousand florins' had been removed from the chests intended for her.[70]

Mary repeatedly reminded Ferdinand that she had dedicated her own assets to ensure his claim to the Hungarian throne and that she expected to be repaid. In March 1527, she explained to Ferdinand that she had been forced to borrow 5,000 ducats on his behalf, stating bluntly, 'I borrowed this sum to serve you,' and emphasising her vulnerability in warning him that she would personally incur 'shame and pity' if Ferdinand did not send her the funds to cover the debt.[71] By April, the sum that Mary wrote about had reached 8,000 ducats and in May, she asserted again that these debts related to her work on her brother's behalf:

> [S]eeing that what I have done has been to serve you, please see to it that I can
> keep what I have promised, because if you do not aid me in this, I will be
> constrained to pay it with my rings or the plate that I use every day, of which

---

[68] 24 October 1527, 'König Ferdinand I: Schreibt wegen der Pressburger Kleinodien an der Räthe der neiderösterreichischen Raitkammer', *Jahrbuch der Kunsthistorischen Sammlungen des Allerhöchsten Kaiserhauses*, 3 (1885), cxl, no. 3003; and [11–14 November] 1527, 'Inventari der Pressburgishn clainater', *Jahrbuch der Kunsthistorischen Sammlungen des Allerhöchsten Kaiserhauses*, 3 (1885), cxli–ii, nos. 3005–7.

[69] 26 May 1528, in Bauer and Lacroix (eds.), *Die Korrespondenz Ferdinands I*, vol. II, part 2 (1938), p. 219.

[70] M. Hatvani (ed.), *Magyar Történelmi okmánytár a Brusseli orszagos levéltárból és a burgundi könyvtárbol*, 4 vols. (Pest: Monumenta hungarica historica, 1857–8), vol. I (1857), part 2, document 162, pp. 26–32 (p. 28).

[71] 14 March 1527, Bauer and Lacroix (eds.), *Die Korrespondenz Ferdinands I*, vol. II, part 1, pp. 40–1.

I have very little, which I would also be happy to do if I could see that it would benefit you.[72]

In 1539, she itemised the expenses that she had incurred on Ferdinand's behalf both at the time she was in Hungary and since, including claims in a memorandum that 'at Pozsony Ferdinand, the king, advanced from our moveable goods cups of gold and of silver, and others gems, to the value of 25,000 Hungarian florins still unrepaid'.[73] Mary's documentation demonstrated her sense of the financial contribution and political labour she had committed to Habsburg victory over at least some of the former kingdom of Hungary. Devotion to her brother and to the Habsburg agenda was expressed in Mary's letters, but she also drew Ferdinand's attention to her own needs and urged respect for her honour. Writing to princes as a younger sister, but also as an engaged political operative for the Habsburg dynasty, required a carefully crafted presentation of feminine modesty, forceful emotions, and steely determination to return again and again to the aspects that mattered to her, whether these were political or financial.

Mary's time in Hungary during the 1520s had contributed markedly to a vital development in the course of the Italian Wars. In the face of a striking disaster and imminent threats from powerful political agents in the region, she had ensured that the Habsburgs retained a large stake in the former kingdom and, through Ferdinand, expanded their direct control over its assets. Ferdinand himself acknowledged Mary's contribution when he wrote on 29 December 1526 that she had 'spared no effort, advice and work of her own or of her followers in order for us to secure the crown and royal title of the Kingdom of Hungary'.[74] Mary's work on the ground in Hungary – her networking labours among the Hungarian elite, employing her own financial resources and those of the Hungarian kingdom, and through her perceptive situation reports to her Habsburg kin on local politics – was pivotal. She guaranteed that the dynasty was still in a position to fight in the region. Ferdinand's holdings in Habsburg Hungary now formed a vital geographical buffer between the Ottomans and his archducal territories in Austria, and were a significant source of resources for the dynasty's ongoing military conflicts across Europe and the Mediterranean.

Mary was not alone among the Habsburg women in managing the finances of their regions for the good of the dynasty. For example, Charles soon realised that his aunt Margaret's competent administration of the Low Countries delivered a powerful boost to his war coffers through her taxation policies, development of

---

[72] 8 May 1527, Bauer and Lacroix (eds.), *Die Korrespondenz Ferdinands I*, vol. II, part 1, p. 66.
[73] Hatvani (ed.), *Magyar Történelmi*, vol. I, part 2, p. 29.
[74] Hatvani (ed.), *Magyar Történelmi*, vol. I, part 1, document 33, p. 50.

textile manufacturing, and trade relations with England.[75] Similarly, the careful oversight by his wife, Isabel of Portugal, of the finances of the Spanish kingdoms enabled Habsburg military campaigns but also allowed for her intervention advising on the military engagements that she identified as key.[76] Preparation to resist a naval attack from corsairs was a key focus of Isabel's activities during this period. In December 1529, she sent Charles an encrypted letter about the serious danger to their realms' Mediterranean coasts and asked him to pay particular attention to her request for aid. Isabel proposed a proactive plan – the urgent organisation of a naval force to be operational within months – that she saw as more beneficial than responsive, intermittent support to affected areas.[77] Isabel voiced a distinct perspective on how military success was to be achieved. She disagreed, for example, in February 1530, with admiral Andrea Doria's request for forty galleys to launch against the Moors: 'the cost could not be borne and it would have little effect'. Isabel argued to Charles that 'the true remedy' was to conquer Algiers and to remove the major corsair of imperial concern, Hızır Hayrettin, from its leadership, for which she suggested both naval and military forces were required.[78] To raise the funds needed for these extensive engagements, Isabel wrote to the realms' leading men to corral support for the building of the armada she envisaged.[79] She was by no means idle in demonstrating her efforts to achieve the necessary organisation and logistical support that such an undertaking demanded. She ordered civic authorities to purchase 3,000 bushels of wheat and employed the funds derived from a papal bull of the Crusade to attend to the defence of the African *presidios*, the expenses of galleys, and the release of captives.[80] However, in September, she feared that their preparations were not yet sufficient, telling Charles: 'We need to start preparing the equipment that the fleet will need immediately, because otherwise it will not be ready in time for next

---

[75] L. Attreed, 'Gender, patronage, and diplomacy in the early career of Margaret of Austria (1480–1530)', *Mediterranean Studies*, 20.1 (2012), 3–27; A.-J.-G. Le Glay (ed.), *Correspondance de l'empereur Maximilien Ier et de Marguerite d'Autriche, sa fille, gouvernante des Pays Bas, de 1507–1519*, 2 vols. (Paris: J. Renouard et Cie, 1839), vol. I; J. de Iongh (ed.), *Margaret of Austria: Regent of the Netherlands* (New York: W. W. Norton, 1953); see the chapter 'Dominium politicum et regale in a composite monarchy: The regencies of Margaret of Austria', in H. G. Koenigsberger, *Monarchies, States Generals and Parliaments: The Netherlands in the Fifteenth and Sixteenth Centuries* (Cambridge: Cambridge University Press, 2001), pp. 93–122.

[76] M. del C. Mazarío Coleto, *Isabel de Portugal, Emperatriz y Reina de España* (Madrid: Escuela de Historia Moderna, 1951); I. Jiménez Zamora, 'La Emperatriz Isabel de Portugal y el Gobierno de la Monarquía Hispánica en tiempos de Carlos V (1526–1539)', unpublished PhD thesis, Universidad Nacional de Educación a Distancia (2015).

[77] Jiménez Zamora, 'La actuación política de la Emperatriz Isabel', p. 171; M. Reder Gadow, 'Isabel de Portugal, Gobernadora De Los Reines de Espana y su proyección de Málaga', *Cuadernos de historia moderna*, 43.2 (2018), 395–423.

[78] 25 February 1530, in Mazarío Coleto, *Isabel de Portugal*, p. 264.

[79] Jiménez Zamora, 'La actuación política de la Emperatriz Isabel', p. 171.

[80] Reder Gadow, 'Isabel de Portugal', pp. 409, 411, 413.

summer's campaigning season.'[81] In 1532, Isabel was again writing to Spain's leading nobles and clerics to arrange preparations, as well as warning the cities of the region such as Málaga to prepare with defences and weapons.[82] Isabel's energy and attention to detail regarding financial, logistical, and military matters ensured that the Habsburgs could continue to take the fight to their enemies.

Resisting the Patriarch

Marriage negotiations highlighted the expectations and realities of wielding dynastic authority. Determining the marriage partners of the dynasty's children was ultimately the role of fathers or father figures, yet women could play an important role in negotiating matches. When Mary's aunt Margaret and her brother Ferdinand suggested new marriages for the young widow, Mary expressed a strong desire not to remarry. She asked instead to be allowed to reside at Ferdinand's court in Vienna. Mary had commissioned a golden heart pendant that she later described in her will:

> Having worn, since the death of my husband, the king, may he rest in peace, a gold heart that he wore until his death, I order that this heart with the chain it hangs on, be melted down and what it is worth given to the poor. For it was the companion of two people until their death, two people who although they were separated from each other for a long time physically, were never so in their love and affection. For this reason, let it be consumed and lose form just as did the bodies of those who loved each other so well.[83]

Mary's image of herself in text, as in portraiture, as an ever-loving and grieving widow supported her desire for bodily autonomy and, with no children from her marriage to protect and guide to adulthood, her identity, loyalty, and orientation could be completely made in terms of her Habsburg origins (Figure 6). After the death of Margaret of Austria in late 1530, Mary accepted Charles' invitation to become her aunt's replacement in the Netherlands, as well as guardian of her nieces, Dorothea and Christina of Denmark, the daughters of her sister Isabella and Christian II of Denmark.[84] However, in appointing Mary governor in the Netherlands, Charles retained firm oversight of her authority by directing her to dismiss the household retinue she had drawn upon in her previous role and to

---

[81] 16 September 1530, in Mazarío Coleto, *Isabel de Portugal*, pp. 292–5; translated in Parker, *Emperor*, p. 234.

[82] Jiménez Zamora, 'La actuación política de la Emperatriz Isabel', p. 173.

[83] Testament of Mary of Hungary, 3 December 1555, *Jahrbuch der Kunsthistorischen Sammlungen des Allerhöchsten Kaiserhauses*, 11 (1890), lxvii, no. 6477.

[84] L. Geevers, 'The Danish Habsburgs: Hans, Dorothea and Christina of Denmark as part of the Habsburg dynasty', in E. Bodensten, K. Brilkman, D. L. Heidenblad, and H. Sanders (eds.), *Nordens Historiker: En vänbok till Harald Gustafsson* (Lund: Historiska institutionen, Lunds Universitet, 2018), pp. 273–86.

Figure 6 Frans Huys (printmaker), Portrait of Mary of Hungary, 1546–62, engraving on paper, 198 mm x 162 mm, Hieronymus Cock (publisher). Rijksmuseum, Amsterdam, RP-P-1881-A-4797

employ Netherlanders of whom he approved.[85] Analysis of Mary's subsequent correspondence with Charles has demonstrated her struggles to quell opposing voices in the region, but of working within the patriarchal constraints imposed by her brother.[86]

With Eleanor nearby as queen of France, the sisters now worked together to advance the dynasty, employing ideas about family relationships to enmesh themselves in political affairs. They hoped to meet in person. Charles expressed misgivings, primarily that the French would use the opportunity to persuade Mary of their claims. Eleanor sought to assuage him, reassuring his ambassador that the meeting was simply 'for the pleasure and contentment between two sisters, who have not seen each other since a very young age, and being in countries so close to each other, it would seem strange if they did not try to visit each other' while Mary's ambassador reassured all that the meeting was no more that 'an amiable visit between two Queens'.[87] This framing of the event as one of family reunion was a convenient fiction, for the eventual meeting at Cambrai in August 1531 was also attended by François and many of the French

---

[85] Parker, *Emperor*, p. 215.   [86] See studies cited at footnote 3.

[87] Boom, *Archiduchesse Éléonore*, p. 108, translated in Knecht, 'Eléonore d'Autriche', pars. 17–18.

court's leading men and women, and arrangements of its ceremonial details were planned by Charles in correspondence with his ambassador.[88]

Establishing peace and recognising alliances were the stated purpose of many Habsburg (and other) marriages during the Wars. Mary and Eleanor set to work from their positions providing further opportunities for diplomatic discussions framed as family get-togethers. In October 1538, the sisters met again at Compiègne, where Habsburg and Valois delegations agreed to a conclusion to the latest phase of hostilities between François and Charles. Contemporaries understood the sisters' influence as critical, the English ambassador writing that Eleanor 'was the principal instrument for managing these interviews. No one knows her brother better than her'.[89] The sisters were uniquely placed go-betweens, and their expressed desire for sorority served an important purpose in staging events across the conflict's opposing sides.

From her position in the Low Countries, Mary proved time and again a valuable asset to Charles' wartime control of an empire. Despite her repeated requests, he did not accept her resignation until 1555, only after he had announced his own resignation as emperor. Soon after, however, he was pressuring her to reprise the role, this time to support her nephew Philip, insisting that should she not return to the Netherlands to govern in Philip's absence, the burden of failure would rest upon her: 'You must not permit the loss in our lifetime of the honour and patrimony that we inherited from our parents and our ancestors, and which we have preserved at the cost of so many and such great trials.' He added the personalised touch of a holograph postscript in which he told Mary, as he later relayed to his daughter Joanna, that 'the salvation – or the loss, dishonour and ruin – of my son the king and of our dynasty depend on her'.[90] Maria José Rodriguez-Salgado has suggested that Charles 'showed little affection for any of them; the most salient characteristic is his desire to control them'.[91] However, this could also be interpreted as a textbook operation of the patriarchal dynastic system. After all, a key feature of early modern dynasties was, as Liesbeth Geevers and Mirella Marini suggest, to embed individuals within a collective narrative that sought to inspire obligations to maintain or advance the dynasty's position, although how far these were 'shared interests', as they write, or those

---

[88] Knecht, 'Eléonore d'Autriche', par. 19.
[89] Boom, *Archiduchesse Éléonore*, p. 126, translated in Knecht, 'Eléonore d'Autriche', par. 22.
[90] Charles to Joanna, 27 August 1558, in Gachard (ed.), *Retraite et mort de Charles-Quint*, vol. I (1854), p. xlv; translated in Parker, *Emperor*, p. 216.
[91] M. J. Rodriguez-Salgado, 'Charles V and the dynasty', in H. Soly (ed.), *Charles V 1500–1558 and His Time* (Antwerp, Mercartorfonds, 1999), pp. 27–111 (p. 56); translated in Parker, *Emperor*, p. 211.

of the male leader, seems open to analysis within individual dynasties and contexts.[92]

Occasionally, women could resist the determinations made by the dynasty's patriarch, at least in small measures. Marriage had very different consequences for the women and men who were expected to conform to dynastic and political logics. Mary of Hungary pushed back against the negotiations that Charles had made to betroth their young niece Christina of Denmark to Francesco Sforza, the duke of imperial controlled Milan from 1521, a man some twenty-seven years older than the eleven-year-old child. Mary, who had been responsible for raising Christina and her siblings after the death of their mother, Isabella, directed her critique to Charles through the lens of his paternal duties and protection of the girl: 'Our niece regards you as her lord and father, in whom she places her entire trust . . . [S]he is only 11 1/ 2, and it is against both God and good sense to marry so young . . . [As] yet she shows no sign of being a woman . . . if she becomes pregnant before she is fully developed you will put both her and the child at risk.'[93] Although the couple were married by proxy in September 1533, Mary refused to allow Christina to join her husband until the following May, when Christina had reached age twelve. Francesco died in November 1535 and the marriage was childless. Mary framed her resistance in terms of reproductive insurance of the dynasty, but she was also protecting a young woman vulnerable to exploitation in the politics of war.

In Summary

The Habsburg call on female relatives to act as regents, diplomats, fundraisers, and strategists during the conflict continued with the dynasty's next generation of patriarchs. When both Charles and Philip were elsewhere in the empire in 1548 to 1551, married cousins, Maria (Charles' daughter) and Maximilian (Ferdinand's eldest son), were called upon to act as regents in the Spanish kingdoms. Philip continued the familialist policy of his father, employing his recently widowed sister, Joanna of Austria, Princess of Portugal, as his regent (in his stead as regent for their father, Charles V) in the Spanish kingdoms when he travelled to England to meet his new bride, Mary I, in 1554.

Family members were considered trustworthy because the affective bonds of familial relationships were seen to hold powerful meaning and they operated as a key language of pressure to enforce compliance. Habsburg women created their own expressions of their status and the complexities of their dynastic identities.

---

[92] Geevers and Marini (eds.), *Dynastic Identity in Early Modern Europe*; see especially 'Introduction: Aristocracy, dynasty and identity in early modern Europe, 1520–1700', pp. 18–35 (p. 19), and further discussion about the role of other family members in shaping family identity (p. 21).

[93] Mary to Charles, 25 August 1533, in Gorter-van Royen and Hoyois (eds.), *Correspondance de Marie de Hongrie avec Charles Quint*, vol. II, pp. 282–5; translated in Parker, *Emperor*, p. 215.

They commissioned visual representations that presented them as capable and vital political players. It is notable that they defined themselves in clothing and in portraits in terms of their status as childless widows, which facilitated interpretations about their exclusive devotion and dedication to their natal dynasty. Letters too were key sites where women negotiated with fathers and brothers, often through articulations of the family responsibilities of patriarchs and male relatives, about their position of power and work on behalf of the dynasty. That they bolstered their male kin in so many ways was well understood by contemporaries. The importance of that support is suggested beautifully by the depiction of key women as the prayer group who accompany Charles V for eternity in the painted depiction of the family in the Basilica of San Lorenzo del Escorial in Madrid (Figure 4).

2 Staging War: Women Producing Valois Masculinity

Unlike in the Habsburg empire, the territorial holdings of the French kingdom were not widely dispersed geographically, and a courtly structure predominated as the French model of power. Authority was concentrated in the person of the monarch, always a man, supported by his leading courtiers in a council. It was nominally only in exceptional circumstances that women, most often female kin, acted as regents in the king's absence, even if this occurred with some regularity during the Italian Wars.[94] Yet wives, mothers, and mistresses were central to French kings' assertions of power. They were crucial diplomatic protagonists and vitally involved in the court's literary and cultural activities. Moreover, through their presence in the royal entourage, ladies of the court drew attention to the king's bodily vigour, sexual attractiveness, and reproductive prowess, essential elements of the martial persona that a successful monarch had to adopt, especially in a time of war.

This section focuses on the political work of Marguerite de Navarre in advancing the French war endeavour, as well as her literary critiques of the cultural, religious, and sexual politics of her elite contemporaries, many of whose lives and attitudes were profoundly marked by the conflicts. Marguerite was the older sister of François I who became France's king in 1515. Born Marguerite d'Angoulême, the daughter of Charles, Duke of Angoulême, then heir to the French throne, she was carefully educated alongside her brother under the guidance of their mother, Louise de Savoie. In 1509, at seventeen, she was married to Charles IV, Duke of Alençon, a soldier engaged in Louis XII's Italian campaigns who had little interest in her intellectual and cultural pursuits. Following François' accession to the throne, Marguerite therefore spent much of her time at her brother's court.

---

[94] See D. Potter, *Renaissance France at War* (Woodbridge: Boydell and Brewer, 2008), pp. 42–62.

Bodies Make the Man

In wars that were narrated as conflicts between individual men, it was critical to assure onlookers of the strong, personal qualities of leaders and their opponents. Charles V was reputed for his intense religiosity; François emphasised his sexual prowess. During his reign, therefore, women's presence and their bodies emerged as vital markers of the king's masculinity. So important was women's attendance at the meeting of the Valois and Tudor monarchs at the Field of the Cloth of Gold in 1520 that the date of the meeting was arranged to accommodate the imminent delivery of François' queen, Claude de France. Her heavily pregnant body bore witness to François' reproductive success in siring sons, a counterpoint to Henry and Katherine's inability to produce a male heir for the Tudor dynasty.[95] Present likewise was François' current sexual companion, Françoise de Foix, who symbolically asserted the French king's virile masculinity.[96] In such ways, the meeting was marked by attention to the bodies of leading women whose distinct activities each made meaning and power for male protagonists. After his stinging defeat by Charles at the Battle of Pavia in 1525 which led to his captivity in Spain, François' claims to a successful martial persona were weak, making his heterosexual conquests even more important to flaunt.

Publicising his non-marital sexual relations could also do other useful work for François, communicating messages about his political allegiances. The king's second marriage to Eleanor, Charles V's sister, was one of the terms of the Treaty of Cambrai. François made sure that, during the associated entry of his new queen, Eleanor, into Paris, he was seen at the window alongside his current companion, Anne de Pisseleu d'Heilly, Duchess d'Étampes, a powerful courtly influencer in her own right.[97] However, claims for François' masculinity were not only made through his own activities and behaviour towards women. They were also supported and extended by the women in his family. The sexual relationship of the unlikely royal couple was material to international relations, and Marguerite was seen as a key source for insights. The Duke of Norfolk, Henry VIII's eyes at the French court, reported that Marguerite had told him 'no man can be worse content with his wife than her brother is, "so that these seven months

---

[95] S. Fisher, 'Queens consort, gender and diplomacy: Catherine of Aragon, Claude of France and the Field of Cloth of Gold', *Gender & History* 35.2 (2022), 387–407.

[96] On the development of the position of royal mistress, see T. Adams and C. Adams, *The Creation of the French Royal Mistress: From Agnès Sorel to Madame Du Barry* (University Park: Pennsylvania State University Press, 2020).

[97] Sir Francis Bryan to Henry VIII [1531], *State Papers*, King Henry the Eight, Part V, Foreign Correspondence, 11 vols. ([London]: [His Majesty's Commission for State Papers], 1830–52), vol. VII: 1527–37 (1849), p. 291.

he neither lay with her, nor yet meddled with her"'.[98] Marguerite's information was made in a context in which François' respect for his wives was understood by courtiers and diplomatic personnel to be conveyed through his interest in sleeping with them. During François' marriage to his first wife, Claude, the secretary of Cardinal Luigi of Aragon, for example, had recorded that 'it is a matter of common report that he holds his wife the Queen in such honour and respect that when in France and with her he has never failed to sleep with her each night'.[99] The visibility of women at court, and the manner in which the king treated them, helped to construct François' hypersexual masculine persona as well as broadcast his political views.

Familial Love as Political Safeguard

Marguerite and her brother, together with the siblings' mother, Louise de Savoie, formed a tight-knit unit known as the Trinity, which operated and was framed as both an emotional and political intimacy (Figure 7). Although she held no official role in François' government, Marguerite was widely understood by foreign

(a)					(b)

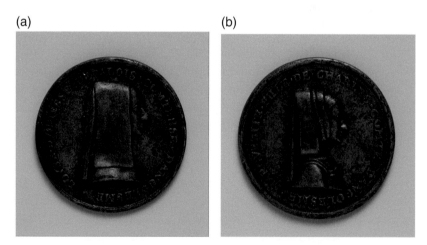

Figure 7 a. Medal of Louise de Savoie; b. Marguerite de Valois, cast *c*.1505; bronze, diameter 60 mm. Harris Brisbane Dick Fund, 1936, Metropolitan Museum of Art, New York, Accession Number 36.110.8

---

[98] Duke of Norfolk to Henry VIII, no. 692, 'Henry VIII: June 1533, 21–25', in *Letters and Papers, Foreign and Domestic, Henry VIII*, 12 vols. (London, 1862–1910), vol. VI, ed. J. Gairdner (1882): '1533', *British History Online*, www.british-history.ac.uk/letters-papers-hen8/vol6/pp306-313.

[99] *The Travel Journal of Antonio de Beatis: German, Switzerland, the Low Countries, France and Italy, 1517–1518*, trans. J. R. Hale and J. M. A. Lindon, ed. J. R. Hale (London: Hakluyt Society, 1979), p. 107.

diplomats as an important conduit to his political thinking. She was deemed by one Venetian ambassador to be a 'woman of great value and great spirit, who participates in all the councils', 'the wisest woman, not only of all the women in France but also of all the men ... in the affairs of state, one can hear no discussion more certain than hers'.[100] When Eleanor of Austria married François in 1530, Margaret of Austria insisted the bride pay particular attention to Marguerite de Navarre: 'she must gain the love of the sister of the King, for she has great credit with him'.[101] Significantly, the king's sister and mother also formed part of his entourage at the Field of the Cloth of Gold.

Marguerite never served as regent within the French kingdom, but it was not unimaginable for a sister to take on such a role at the French court. The first French king to lead troops on campaign as part of the Wars, Charles VIII, had left his kingdom in the care of his elder sister, Anne de France, and her husband, Pierre de Beaujeu, when he marched French troops and Swiss mercenaries into battle to assert his claim to the throne of Naples. Charles' confidence to leave his kingdom in the hands of his closest blood relative reflected the success of an earlier regency. Twenty-two-year-old Anne had already acted in this role alongside her husband from the time Charles had ascended to the throne as a thirteen-year-old in 1481 until he came of age in 1491.

Valois kings continued to utilise women connected to them by blood as official regents during military absences. François I appointed his mother, Louise de Savoie, regent, first when he was on campaign in 1515 which achieved the taking of Milan, and in 1525–6 when he was captured and taken to Madrid as the prisoner of Charles V after the Battle of Pavia.[102] As noted in Section 1, on her son's behalf, Louise negotiated the Treaty of Cambrai, or 'Ladies' Peace,' with Margaret of Austria.[103] In that diplomatic moment, it was the fact that Margaret and Louise were seen to have no other objectives than the best outcome for their nephew and son respectively, that made them suitable negotiators. Envoy from the French court, Gilbert Bayard, sieur de Font, assured Margaret that François would respect the

---

[100] F. Giustianian, 1537, in N. Tommaseo (ed.), *Relations des ambassadeurs vénitiens sur les affaires de France au XVIe siècle*, 2 vols. (Paris: Imprimerie royale, 1838), vol. I, p. 172; M. Dandolo in A. Baschet, *La diplomatie vénitienne: Les princes de l'Europe au XVIe siècle* (Paris: Plon, 1862), p. 412.

[101] 21 July 1530, in Boom, *Archiduchesse Éléonore,* p. 96; translated in Knecht, 'Eléonore d'Autriche', par. 14.

[102] A. David-Chapy, 'The political, symbolic, and courtly power of Anne de France and Louise de Savoie: from genesis to the glory of female regency', and L. Fagnart and M. B. Winn, 'Louise de Savoie: The king's mother, alter rex', in Broomhall (ed.), *Women and Power at the French Court*, pp. 43–64 and 85–114; P. Brioist, L. Fagnart, and C. Michon (eds.), *Louise de Savoie (1476–1531)* (Tours: Presses universitaires François-Rabelais, 2015).

[103] See new assessments of this peace in Dumont, Fagnart, Le Roux, and Girault (eds.), *La Paix des Dames, 1529.*

outcome fashioned by them because 'there was no other third part in whom he can have or take better cause or foundation to agree' than his mother.[104]

Marguerite's letters to her brother reveal her equally important role in the Trinity as an intermediary between mother and son, supporting her mother's activities and informing the king about their work during Louise's later regency.[105] Their correspondence also sustained the siblings' shared enjoyment of intellectual life, creating space for poetic exchange and religious expression. It was Marguerite rather than Louise, whose role anchored her to the court, who was able to act as physical go-between when she travelled to Spain to visit her brother and advance the negotiations that would see François' eventual release in March 1526.

Alliances of Faith

At the 1520 meeting on the Field of the Cloth of Gold, Marguerite developed a strong relationship with the English cardinal Thomas Wolsey, so close indeed that she was referred to as Wolsey's 'daughter by adoption'.[106] Marguerite's broad support for closer ties between France and England at this period provided English officials with a significant mediating presence close to the French king. Her own interest was no doubt shaped by Henry VIII's break from Rome, for Marguerite also began to engage with the idea of religious reform. In the early 1520s, she corresponded with the bishop of Meaux, Guillaume Briçonnet, and a circle of intellectuals, exchanging views and refining their positions on evangelical theology and potential reforms.[107]

Although Marguerite's influence would wax and wane in the competitive environment of the French court, in the 1540s, she was able to collaborate around shared evangelical interests with François' favoured companion, the Duchess d'Étampes, who was perhaps the kingdom's most influential Huguenot.[108]

---

[104] Le Glay (ed.), *Négociations diplomatiques*, vol. II, p. 683.

[105] A. Champollion-Figeac, *Captivité du roi François Ier* (Paris: Imprimerie royale, 1847); A. Champollion-Figeac (ed.), *Poésies, et correspondance intime du roi avec Diane de Poitiers et plusieurs autres dames de la cour du roi François Ier, de Louise de Savoie, duchesse d'Angoulême, de Marguerite, reine de Navarre* (Geneva: Slatkine, 1847; 1970).

[106] Etienne de Poncher, archbishop of Sens, to Wolsey, 13 July 1520, no. 912, 'Henry VIII: July 1520, 1–15', in *Letters and Papers, Foreign and Domestic, Henry VIII*, 12 vols. (London, 1862–1910), vol. III, ed. J. S. Brewer (1867): '1519–1523', *British History Online*, www.british-history.ac.uk/letters-papers-hen8/vol3/pp320-331.

[107] B. Stephenson, *The Power and Patronage of Marguerite de Navarre* (Aldershot: Ashgate, 2004); J. A. Reid, *King's Sister – Queen of Dissent: Marguerite of Navarre (1492–1549) and Her Evangelical Network*, 2 vols. (Leiden: Brill, 2009); and J. A. Reid, 'Imagination and influence: The creative powers of Marguerite de Navarre at work at court and in the world', in Broomhall (ed.), *Women and Power at the French Court*, pp. 263–86.

[108] D. Potter, 'Politics and faction at the court of Francis I: The Duchesse d'Étampes, Montmorency and the Dauphin Henri', *French History*, 21.2 (2007), 127–46; D. Potter, 'The life and after-life of a royal mistress: Anne de Pisseleu, Duchess of Étampes', in Broomhall (ed.), *Women and Power at the French Court*, pp. 309–34.

Approached by diplomats to intercede and persuade the king, or at least to know his views, Marguerite helped to reorient François' diplomatic endeavours in that decade towards alignment with Protestants such as the Lutheran princes of the Holy Roman Empire who had allied in the Schmalkaldic League.[109]

Marguerite's religious activities continued a long history of engagement by the court's leading women with literature, piety, and pedagogy. The importance women placed on educating young women to be valuable and valued interlocutors in courtly politics was documented in a work written by Anne de France for her daughter Suzanne.[110] Both Anne de Bretagne and her daughter Claude had as queen accumulated extensive libraries that emphasised the high value they placed on women's learning, of which pious texts formed an important part.[111] Claude developed a particular interest in religious reform that contemporaries noted as offering an alternative politics to that of her husband, François.[112] Her sister, Renée, who later became Duchess of Ferrara, would eventually be sent by her husband to what he hoped was seclusion at the rural court of Consandolo to prevent her from assisting both Protestants and her French relatives.[113] Marguerite, in her turn, sponsored literary endeavours and discussion of religious reform, but like that other influential sister of a king, Anne de France, she also produced her own works. Marguerite created a vast range of work over her lifetime across many genres, much of which focused on religious themes and tended towards the mystic in her later life. Marguerite cultivated a wide circle of humanist and evangelical correspondents, women and men, across Europe, with whom she discussed spiritual matters.[114] It was to be her evangelical works that gained visible traction among a community of women as they were translated into English and circulated among that court's elite women where its messages would find a receptive home. Anne Boleyn, who had once been a lady-in-waiting to Claude, owned a copy of Marguerite's *Mirror of a Sinful Soul*, which Anne's daughter, Elizabeth, translated into English as a gift for her

---

[109] Reid, *King's Sister*, vol. II, pp. 505–71; Stephenson, *Power and Patronage*, pp. 149–83.

[110] M. A. Chazaud (ed.), *Les enseignements d'Anne de France, duchesse de Bourbonnois et d'Auvergne, à sa fille Susanne de Bourbon* (Moulins: Desrosiers, 1878); Anne of France, *Lessons for my Daughter*, trans. and ed. S. L. Janson (Cambridge: D. S. Brewer, 2012).

[111] K. Wilson-Chevalier and E. Pascal (eds.), *Patronnes et mécènes en France à la Renaissance* (Sainte-Etienne: Presses universitaires de Saint-Etienne, 2007); C. J. Brown (ed.), *The Cultural and Political Legacy of Anne de Bretagne: Negotiating Convention in Books and Documents* (Woodbridge: Boydell and Brewer, 2010).

[112] K. Wilson-Chevalier, 'Claude de France and the spaces of agency of a marginalized queen', in Broomhall (ed.), *Women and Power at the French Court*, pp. 139–72.

[113] K. D. Peebles and G. Scarlatta (eds.), *Representing the Life and Legacy of Renée de France: From Fille de France to Dowager Duchess* (Cham: Springer, 2021).

[114] See, for example, with Vittoria Colonna, B. Collett, *A Long and Troubled Pilgrimage: The Correspondence of Marguerite d'Angoulême and Vittoria Colonna, 1540–1545* (Princeton, NJ: Princeton Theological Seminary, 2000).

stepmother, Catherine Parr. In such ways, women's spiritual, pedagogical, and literary cultures extended across polities in reflection and support of political alliances both made and sustained by the Italian Wars.

Writing War

The presence of the Wars and their meaning for French structures of power flowed through cultural forms in multiple ways. Courtly women were important contributors to this project, documenting the experience of war in a range of genres. The journal made by Louise de Savoie, for example, provided an insight into the conflicts as seen from her privileged position at court. Its entries demonstrate her access to knowledge about even distant campaigns, especially those in which her son, François, featured: 'On the 13th September 1515, which was a Thursday, my son vanquished and defeated the Swiss near Milan, the combat commenced at five in the afternoon, and lasted all night until eleven in the morning ... my son, glorious and triumphant Caesar, subjugator of the Swiss.'[115] From her position as an eyewitness to the events of the Field of the Cloth of Gold, she could note how at the mass attended by both François and Henry VIII, 'my son knelt on the right, and took the peace and the gospel first'.[116] When, in 1522, Henry's herald declared in front of François that his master was the French king's mortal enemy, 'my son responded coldly,' recorded Louise, 'and so opportunely that everyone present was delighted and amazed by his clear eloquence.'[117] The topics that formed Louise's journal suggest how an elite woman's experiences of war could be intertwined with that of male kin, as were Louise's with her son, François, as she depicted herself in this text as 'the poor mother, happy to see my son safe and sound after so much violence that he has suffered and sustained to serve the public good'.[118] Louise's journal produced a narrative of the Wars that made men's political and military activities central to women's identities and experiences of these events.

The Wars, and questions of male courtly conduct in times of war and women's role in defining it, found expression in chivalric literature that was profoundly popular at the French court. Perhaps curiously, the most popular of this genre was the Iberian saga, *Amadís de Gaula*, which circulated in

---

[115] Abbé C.-F. Lambert (ed.), 'Journal de Louise de Savoie, duchesse d'Angoulesme, d'Anjou et de Valois, mère du grand roi François premier', in M. Petitot et al. (eds.), *Collection complète des mémoires relatifs à l'histoire de France*, 131 vols. (Paris: Foucault, 1819–29), vol. XVI (1826), 383–408 (p. 398). See also N. Kuperty-Tsur, 'Le *Journal* de Louise de Savoie: Nature et visées', in Brioist, Fagnart, and Michon (eds.), *Louise de Savoie*, pp. 263–76; H. Hauser, 'Le *Journal* de Louise de Savoie', *Revue historique*, 86 (1904), 280–303.

[116] Lambert (ed.), 'Journal de Louise de Savoie', p. 404.

[117] Lambert (ed.), 'Journal de Louise de Savoie', pp. 406–7.

[118] Lambert (ed.), 'Journal de Louise de Savoie', p. 399.

translation across the reigns of François I and his heir, Henri II. The latter pursued a series of campaigns that marked the final phase of the Wars, leading from the front line. Courtly culture in Henri's absence was shaped not only by the regent, his queen Catherine de' Medici, but also by the powerful presence of his long-time companion, Diane de Poitiers. Contemporaries read the complex relationships between these women and their presentation in cultural forms through the lens of works such as *Amadís*, a number of volumes of which were dedicated to Diane.[119] Mars and Venus come together in this chivalric romance that presents elite male knightly behaviour as legible in praiseworthy relationships with women, reflected in particular in a steadfast devotion to a single honoured lady. Neither François nor Henri managed this achievement, but the work also saw its hero conduct sexual relations outside of marriage, all the while courageously undertaking successive battle feats with a group of male comrades.

It was in the context of this environment, and with exposure through the Wars to Italian traditions of literature, that Marguerite wrote her most well-known work, the *Heptaméron*. In the prologue, one of the book's narrators, Parlemente, comments on the interest at court in the recent translation of Boccaccio's *Decameron*, which was 'highly thought of by the [most Christian] King Francis I, by Monseigneur the Dauphin, Madame the Dauphine, and Madame Marguerite'.[120] Baldassare Castiglione's *Book of the Courtier* (1528) was another important influence on Marguerite, the impact of Italian humanism contributing significantly to her vision of contemporary courtly culture. The *Heptaméron*'s Prologue explains that the group of storytellers, stranded in a remote abbey during a devastating flood, agreed to tell stories to pass the time, following Boccaccio's *Decameron* as a model for their activity. The work foregrounds the mixed-sex environments that operated at the French court. However, the presence of war is never far from its pages. What is striking in the tales is their significantly violent nature, often sexual and emotional as well as physical. Many of them depict contemporary figures who were well known at court and their activities take place in the context of the Italian Wars. Conflict therefore forms a backdrop to the stories' discussion of distinct forms of violence experienced by women and men.

---

[119] S. Broomhall, 'Corresponding romances: Henri II and the last campaigns of the Italian Wars', in S. Downes, A. Lynch, and K. O'Loughlin (eds.), *Writing War in Britain and France, 1370–1854: A History of Emotions* (London: Routledge, 2018), pp. 107–25.

[120] Marguerite de Navarre, *The Heptameron*, trans. P. A. Chilton (London, Penguin, 1984; 2004), p. 68. See also C. H. Winn, *Approaches to Teaching Marguerite de Navarre's* Heptaméron (Berkeley, CA: Modern Language Association, 2007); G. Ferguson and M. B. McKinley, 'The *Heptaméron*: Word, spirit, world', in G. Ferguson and M. B. McKinley (eds.), *A Companion to Marguerite de Navarre* (Leiden: Brill, 2013), pp. 323–71.

Women's bodies emerge from the *Heptaméron* as a battleground upon which male honour can be both impugned and asserted. Contemporaries understood women's chastity as an asset that was guarded and exchanged between men, and male honour as demonstrable through sexual success. In the forty-seventh tale, a character thus promises revenge after the breakdown of a male friendship by seducing the other's wife. War also formed the vocabulary of the *Heptaméron*'s discussion of sexual pursuit and conquest. One male discussant, Hircan, suggests to the women in his audience after hearing a tale in which a young woman is raped in her bed by a friar: 'You are not experienced in war and in the use of the stratagems that it requires; among these, one of the most important is to kindle strife in the camp of the enemy, whereby he becomes far easier to conquer.'[121] The sixteenth tale, set during the French occupation of Milan, explores social interactions between a French gentleman and an elite Milanese widow, who, as a member of the defeated population, is obliged to endorse the French victory through her spectatorship and attendance at festivities hosted for the city's governor, Charles II d'Amboise, who did indeed control the city from 1503 to 1511 on behalf of François I. The widow devises a plan to determine the gentleman's willingness to fight for her, by arranging for her brothers to attack him. His gallant response merits the lady's praises: 'You're even more handsome, even more charming and even more valiant than people had told me.'[122] In this tale, a man's readiness to engage in violence, and to accept physical harm as a result, in this case in pursuit of sex, appears to be rendered, perhaps ironically, a kind of chivalric gesture and a virtuous example of elite masculinity.

Female survivors of assault are depicted in the *Heptaméron* experiencing far less favourable outcomes. They often choose silence about their experiences for lack of any form of redress. Nonetheless, while the characters operate within the ideologies of their time, both the *Heptaméron*'s attention to such stories, and the diverse range of responses to them by discussants, are noteworthy. Patricia Cholakian has suggested that the work's focus, and particular tales, may reflect sexual assaults that Marguerite herself experienced.[123] A very detailed depiction of sexual harassment and eventual assault of a young widow, Florida, by a gentleman, Amador, renowned for his wartime exploits, is provided in the tenth tale, which is notably set in Spain, the territory of François' Habsburg rival. Amador pursues Florida with both militarised rhetoric and the argument that he might perish in wartime service, to persuade Florida to succumb to his

---

[121] *The Heptameron of the Tales of Margaret, Queen of Navarre* (London: Gibbings and Company [1898]), Tale 46b (Gruget edition), vol. IV, p. 199.

[122] Marguerite de Navarre, *The Heptameron*, pp. 207–8.

[123] P. Cholakian, *Rape and Writing in the Heptaméron of Marguerite de Navarre* (Carbondale: Southern Illinois University Press, 1991).

desire. There is a hint at the conclusion of the tale that Amador might be a thinly disguised portrait of a well-known figure at the French court. One of the assembled listeners, Geburon, claims to recognise the protagonist, who he then praises as a military hero: 'in my opinion Amador was the most noble and valiant knight that ever lived . . . if it's the man I think it is, then he's a man who never experienced fear in his life, a man whose heart was never devoid of love or the desire for courageous action'.[124] In another tale, a widowed princess devotedly attached to her brother (a profile suspiciously like Marguerite's own), narrowly avoids being assaulted by a friend of her brother. A male respondent critiques her would-be assaulter, who 'lacked nerve, and didn't deserve to have his memory preserved. What an opportunity he had! He should never have been content to eat or sleep till he had succeeded'.[125] The *Heptaméron*'s treatment of male courtly behaviour suggests that an elite manly identity is achieved in wartime through sexual conquest and persuasive rhetorical skills, as well as physical violence.

Marguerite's *Heptaméron* was both a record and reflection of contemporary French courtly culture. It explored how the experience of successive generations of young men sent to war abroad and their engagements – political, cultural, and sexual – with populations there as well as at home were understood through an evolving elite masculinity that demanded military, sexual, and rhetorical prowess in equal measure and assumed that women's bodies were the site through which such prowess could be trained and tested.

In Summary

The bodies and minds of courtly women, as well as men, were vital to the French war effort and to the fortunes of the Valois dynasty. A well-educated, politically sophisticated and highly visible cohort of elite women at the French court served the conflict through their communications, networks, spiritual expression, and cultural reflections about war. In ways that are different from how Habsburg women carried out wartime service, distinct forms of personal intimacy with the monarch as an individual – forms that were familial, emotional, and sexual – marked their contribution. Women appeared particularly important in drawing attention to key aspects of Valois kingship, especially in asserting the virile masculinity of François I. Through Marguerite, the idea of sexual prowess of elite men as martial performance became a matter for debate in one of the century's most significant literary works. The Italian Wars, seen

---

[124] Marguerite de Navarre, *The Heptameron*, p. 154.
[125] Marguerite de Navarre, *The Heptameron*, p. 96.

from a French perspective, therefore, were as much produced through the pens and mouths of women as the swords of men.

3 Surviving War: The Political Work of Italian Princely Consorts

How Italy's elite women engaged in the Italian Wars was fundamentally shaped by the gendered traditions associated with the varying systems of power in the peninsula's republics, principalities, and small lordships. It is almost entirely in the context of Italy's courts that evidence of women's administrative and diplomatic work in support of their menfolk's regimes and military activities is to be found. However, the conflicts impacted on Italy's principalities and southern monarchy to different degrees, some states remaining relatively unscathed, while others, such as the kingdom of Naples, the duchy of Milan and the smaller duchy of Urbino, suffered invasion and multiple regime changes. The archival record concerning the roles of elite Italian women during the Wars reflects these varying experiences. Only a fraction of the correspondence of Elisabetta Gonzaga, the wife of the military captain and Duke of Urbino, Guidobaldo da Montefeltro, remains, for example. The same is true of Elisabetta's niece and successor as Duchess of Urbino, Leonora Gonzaga, whose husband, Francesco Maria della Rovere, was also a prominent mercenary commander. The duchy of Urbino was attacked twice during the Wars and both Elisabetta and Leonora led peripatetic lives during periods of exile. Their crucial activities in provisioning armies and defending the duchy's borders, as well as their diplomacy at the papal court, are thinly documented because of their own mobility and wartime losses to the Montefeltro archives.[126]

Yet the portrait of Elisabetta from circa 1504, attributed to Raphael, in which the duchess is shown at an extraordinarily monumental scale, communicates something of her political significance in the context of the Wars (Figure 8). The portrait likely celebrates the restoration of the Montefeltro regime in Urbino following the death of the Borgia pope, Alexander VI, in 1503. Elisabetta and her husband had spent an anxious time in exile in Venice after being driven from Urbino by the army of the pope's son, Cesare Borgia. The portrait's iconography must be understood in this precise political context. Elisabetta is represented against a misty backdrop of sky and mountains that is recognisably the landscape of the Marches, her upper body entirely filling the lower half of the painting. The magnificent gown features the traditional gold and black colours

---

[126] For one of the few published collections of the women's letters, see A. Mercati, *Lettere di Elisabetta e di Leonora Gonzaga a Francesco Maria della Rovere* (Mantua: Reale Accademia Virgiliana di Mantova, 1941). See also A. Luzio and R. Renier, *Mantova e Urbino: Isabella d'Este ed Elisabetta Gonzaga nelle relazioni familiari e nelle vicende politiche* (Turin: Roux, 1893).

Figure 8 Sanzio Raffaello (Raphael), portrait of Elisabetta Gonzaga, *c*.1504–5; oil on wood, 525 mm x 373 mm. Uffizi Gallery. Alamy

of the Montefeltro dynasty, a reassuring reference to the subject's long loyalty to it, while her heavy-lidded gaze was likely meant to be read as dignified and resolute, communicating an unflinching resolve to represent her husband and to protect his subjects from future crises associated with the Wars.

The portrait, and others like it representing princely spouses, have received surprisingly little scholarly attention. It is as if political image-making during this period is not recognised as such if the subject of a portrait is a woman, while paintings of the Wars' male protagonists in splendid parade armour or mounted on fine horses are readily interpreted as central to their militarist and political self-fashioning.[127] Yet, as we have seen in Sections 1 and 2 in relation to Habsburg and Valois contexts, portraits and other visual artefacts were central to elite Italian women's efforts to shape their public identities as competent and virtuous political deputies who could carry out the administrative and diplomatic work required of them by ruling husbands and sons in the midst of wartime crises.

In this section, we focus on several better-documented women connected to the marquisate of Mantua and the neighbouring duchy of Ferrara, neither of which witnessed the defeat and exile of its ruling house, although these tiny states were certainly not immune to the dangers posed by the Wars. Mantua

---

[127] On this theme, see C. James, 'Political image making in portraits of Isabella d'Este', *Gender & History*, 35.1 (2023), 20–41.

came perilously close to being attacked by Louis XII's army in the early years of the sixteenth century, while the Venetian republic attempted, unsuccessfully as it turned out, to absorb Ferrara into its territory in 1509. The Este faced another crisis in 1512. Pope Julius II was intent on besieging Ferrara and restoring direct papal rule, but he died suddenly in 1513, before he could realise that ambition. The well-preserved Gonzaga and Este archives permit investigation of how the Wars impacted two ruling families with a history of close political cooperation between the princely ruler and his wife and whose other female relatives had traditionally taken an active and occasionally a pivotal role in diplomacy.

States of Power

The political structures of Italy were more diverse than those explored in Sections 1 and 2, and these differences had consequences for how women were involved in the Wars. Italy's republics, for example, actively prevented elite women from assuming a visible role in politics. Indeed, the transition of the Florentine republic to a hereditary principate over the course of the first decades of the sixteenth century, largely the result of the intense political pressures created within the city by the Wars, demonstrates how important the dismantling of republican structures was to the ability of a few women to infiltrate Florence's halls of power.

The first radical change occurred in February 1503, when Argentina Malaspina, daughter of the lord of Fosdinovo, was permitted to move into the Palazzo della Signoria following the appointment of her husband, Piero Soderini, as the republic's gonfalonier of justice, not for the usual two months, but for life.[128] The priors, including the gonfalonier, had previously lived without their wives within the Palazzo della Signoria for the brief term of their appointments. By emulating the stronger culture of continuity in Venice that came with the office of doge, who remained in his position until death, republican authorities hoped to improve their responses to the threats posed by the Wars. However, the sight of women at the windows of the Palazzo della Signoria, and Argentina's expectation that she could sit with her husband when he received ambassadors and openly act as her husband's political collaborator, aroused disgust in contemporary Florentine observers such as the chronicler Bartolomeo Cerretani. He criticised Soderini's tolerance of his wife's presence in political meetings as the behaviour 'not of a gonfalonier, but of a lord'.[129]

---

[128] L. Landucci, *Diario fiorentino dal 1450 al 1516*, ed. Iodoco del Badia (Florence: Studio Biblos, 1969), p. 254; R. Pesman, *Pier Soderini and the Ruling Class in Renaissance Florence* (Goldbach: Keip, 2002), p. 49.

[129] B. Cerretani, *Ricordi*, ed. G. Berti (Florence: Olschki, 1993), p. 84. On the stark contrast in attitudes to elite female involvement in politics in a republic and a principality, see C. James, 'Florence and Ferrara: Dynastic marriage and politics', in R. Black and J. E. Law (eds.), *The*

The blurring of domestic and political spaces that occurred within Florence's Palazzo della Signoria after 1503 was strictly prevented in Venice. While the dogaressa and her female retinue lived within the doge's palace, the women were confined to residential areas of the building and specific laws stopped them from corresponding with anyone who might become part of a political network. Such structural mechanisms proved unnecessary during the Wars because all the doges appointed between 1486 and 1556 were bachelors or widowers. Thus even the ceremonies and processions involving the dogaressa, which had given her significant public visibility in the earlier decades of the fifteenth century, were in abeyance during these decades.[130]

Many citizens measured the sharp decline in Florentine republicanism that followed the Spanish imposition of Medici rule in 1512 in terms of the degree to which the women of the family began to exercise significant influence and even direct authority. Alfonsina Orsini governed Florence on behalf of her son, Lorenzo II di Piero de' Medici, when he led Florentine troops against the French in 1515, and she also acted as the representative in Florence of the Medici pope, Leo X.[131] Later, the regencies of Eleonora di Toledo while her husband, Duke Cosimo I de' Medici, was fighting in the Wars in 1541, 1543, and between 1551 and 1554, were powerful reminders to Florentines that republicanism was extinguished and a hereditary principate now firmly in place.[132]

The increasingly princely culture the Medici imposed on Florence after 1512 also characterised the court of the family's popes, Leo X and Clement VII, who permitted an unprecedented number of female relatives to remain in Rome, where the women lobbied vigorously for political favours.[133] But, even before this time, Alexander VI and Julius II had included female kin in nepotistic attempts to use the Wars to further their dynastic ambitions. In 1499, Pope Alexander VI appointed his daughter Lucrezia Borgia to rule Spoleto and other Umbrian towns on his behalf while he was temporarily absent from the Vatican. He delegated similar responsibilities to her in 1500 and 1501.[134] Alexander VI

Medici: Citizens and Masters (Florence: Villa I Tatti, Harvard University Centre for Italian Renaissance Studies, 2015), pp. 365–78.

[130] H. S. Hurlburt, *The Dogaressa of Venice, 1200–1500: Wife and Icon* (Houndsmills: Palgrave Macmillan, 2006), p. 179.

[131] N. Tomas, 'Alfonsina Orsini de' Medici and the 'problem' of a female ruler in early sixteenth century Florence', *Renaissance Studies*, 14.1 (2000), 70–90.

[132] On this theme, see N. Tomas, 'Eleonora di Toledo, regency and state formation in Tuscany', in G. Benadusi and J. C. Brown (eds.), *Medici Women: The Making of a Dynasty in Grand Ducal Tuscany* (Toronto: Centre for Reformation and Renaissance Studies, 2015), pp. 59–89.

[133] N. Tomas, *The Medici Women, Gender and Power in Renaissance Florence* (Aldershot: Ashgate, 2003), pp. 124–63.

[134] S. Feci, 'Signore di curia: Rapporti di potere ed esperienze di governo nella Roma papale (metà XV–metà XVI secolo)', in L. Arcangeli and S. Peyronel (eds.), *Donne di potere nel Rinascimento* (Rome: Viella, 2008), pp. 195–222 (pp. 219–21).

openly recognised his children and permitted them to frequent the papal court, but his successor Julius II was more cautious. He occasionally invited his daughter, Felice della Rovere, to dine with him in private within his apartments, but she lived elsewhere and had no public prominence in political matters. Yet, once Felice married Gian Giordano Orsini, she was drawn into her father's politicking. In 1511, for example, Julius II made Felice his representative in peace talks with Louis XII. While her husband met with the king, Felice negotiated with the French queen Anne de Bretagne, prefiguring the peacemaking of the female relatives of François I and Charles V, discussed in Section 2.[135] We suggest that the more dynastic a political structure became, the more women as family members became involved in the political fortunes of the dynasty, as exemplified in the duchy of Ferrara and the marquisate of Mantua, explored below in this Element.

Wartime Collaborations between Italian Princely Couples

The political work of Isabella d'Este (1474–1539), who became marchioness of Mantua when she married Francesco Gonzaga in 1490, was the focus of a series of influential essays by the late nineteenth-century archivist Alessandro Luzio. Her artistic and literary patronage has also been exhaustively analysed.[136] Here, we examine that scholarship in a broader frame by situating Isabella's political roles alongside those of two of her sisters-in-law. We argue that the diplomatic work of the marchioness, often considered unique by scholars, was not unusual during the Italian Wars. As we will show, the diplomacy of Clara Gonzaga (1464–1503), whose marriage in 1481 to Gilbert of Montpensier-Bourbon, Count of Aigueperse and leader of Charles VIII's expedition to conquer the kingdom of Naples, placed her at the centre of relations between the French crown, and her brother Francesco's regime in Mantua, was similarly important.[137]

Another of Isabella's sisters-in-law, Lucrezia Borgia (1480–1519), Duchess of Ferrara from 1505, helped to preserve Este rule at two crucial moments

---

[135] Feci, 'Signore di curia', p. 218.

[136] For this extensive scholarship, see the bibliography in C. James, *A Renaissance Marriage: The Political and Personal Alliance of Isabella d'Este and Francesco, 1490–1519* (Oxford: Oxford University Press, 2020). In this monograph, James explores the ups and downs of Isabella's political roles and the pressures the Wars placed on the relationship with her husband. See also S. Cockram, *Isabella d'Este and Francesco Gonzaga: Power Sharing at the Renaissance Court* (Farnham: Ashgate, 2013) and C. Shaw, *Isabella d'Este: A Renaissance Princess* (London: Routledge, 2019).

[137] On Clara Gonzaga, see N. Dupont-Pierrart, *Claire de Gonzague Comtesse de Bourbon-Montpensier (1464–1503): Une princesse italienne à la cour de France* (Lille: Septentrion, 2017) and C. James, 'The diplomacy of Clara Gonzaga, countess of Montpensier-Bourbon: Gendered perspectives of family duty, honour and female agency', *Renaissance Studies*, 35.3 (2020), 486–502.

during the Wars. Her figure is shrouded in the dark myths propagated by enemies of her father, Pope Alexander VI, and brother, Cesare, whose dynastic ambitions embroiled the young Lucrezia in scandals not of her own making. Following her marriage in 1502 to Alfonso I d'Este, heir to the duchy of Ferrara, and especially after her father and brother died in 1503 and 1507 respectively, Lucrezia was able to put the ruthless machinations of her male relatives behind her. Recent scholarship associated with a critical edition of her extant letters has shown Lucrezia in a new light, one in which she is not a helpless political pawn of the Borgia men, but rather a savvy diplomatic and entrepreneurial actor whose activities supported Alfonso's ability to remain in power.[138]

The expectation that a prince's wife would assist her husband as his political deputy was well established in Italy long before the Italian Wars began.[139] Indeed, we find an explicit statement about these duties in a letter that Isabella d'Este's mother, Eleonora d'Aragona, Duchess of Ferrara and eldest daughter of the king of Naples, sent to her recently married daughter in April 1491.

> You well know that whoever has a husband, and a state, must also have many duties, keeping in mind that you must produce children, and it is necessary to look after them and conserve their possessions and the state, as well as to do those things which are necessary for your subjects and citizens, whenever it is required.[140]

Although service to the marital dynasty is foregrounded here, Eleonora took it for granted that her daughter would always keep her natal family's interest firmly in view, as she herself had done by mediating the often-vexed political relationship between her father and husband. Isabella's diplomatic efforts to navigate family loyalties once the Gonzaga and Este rulers were forced to take diverging paths in their efforts to survive the Wars proved complex.

Only seventeen when she obeyed her mother and began to help her husband by lightening his administrative load, Isabella proved a competent deputy, as Francesco Gonzaga enthusiastically acknowledged in a letter to his sister Clara: 'I can hardly refrain from telling your Ladyship that during our absence

---

[138] D. Y. Ghirardo (ed.), *Lucrezia Borgia Lettere 1494–1519* (Mantua: Direzione generale Archivi, Tre Lune Edizioni, 2020).

[139] On the diplomacy and administrative roles of Isabella d'Este's mother, Eleonora d'Aragona, see V. Prisco, *Eleonora d'Aragona: Pratiche di potere e modelli culturali nell' Italia del Rinascimento* (Rome: Viella, 2022); J. O'Leary, 'Politics, pedagogy, and praise: Three literary texts dedicated to Eleonora d'Aragona', *I Tatti Studies in the Italian Renaissance*, 19.2 (2016), 285–307; James, 'Florence and Ferrara'. See also J. O'Leary, *Elite Women As Diplomatic Agents in Italy and Hungary, 1470–1510* (Leeds: ARC Humanities Press, 2022); On Mantua, see E. W. Swain, '"My excellent and most singular lord": Marriage in a noble family of fifteenth-century Italy', *Journal of Medieval and Renaissance Studies*, 16 (1986), 171–95.

[140] 15 April 1491, in James, *A Renaissance Marriage*, p. 56, n. 12.

we have left the burden and governance of our state and dominion to our illustrious consort, knowing that we can well rely on her prudence and integrity, for even if she is still of tender age, she has shown great promise.'[141] In this period, Francesco's absences from Mantua were brief, occasioned for the most part by visits to his country estates and several diplomatic expeditions further afield. However, with the French invasion of 1494, he was obliged to fulfil his contract as a military captain for the republic of Venice. Isabella assumed increasingly weighty political responsibilities, while Francesco devoted himself to fighting. Over time, her administrative and diplomatic work came to exceed that of her predecessors, as the crises generated by war forced a more and more radical interpretation of how political collaboration between husband and wife should look.

Isabella's letters reveal how well attuned she was to the challenges that foreign invasion and the proximity of war to urban populations presented to Italy's rulers. The shockingly rapid capitulation of the Aragonese regime in Naples to Charles VIII's army in February 1495 was a sobering example of what could happen, even to a monarch whose hold on power seemed secure. On learning the news about the fall of Naples to the French, Isabella wrote to Francesco, expressing utter amazement, but also vowing to take to heart the lesson offered by the Neapolitan debacle: 'This case must serve as an example to all the lords and potentates of the world to take more account of their subjects' hearts than of fortresses, treasure, and men-at-arms, since the discontent of subjects prompts a worse war than any enemy to be found beyond city walls.'[142] Only a few months later, Isabella's resolve was put to the test. Civic unrest broke out in Mantua, sparked by merchants preferring to supply grain at inflated prices to the army of the Italian League rather than to city markets. Placards bemoaning the shortage of bread appeared overnight on the walls of buildings around central piazzas. In response, Isabella quickly lifted the ceiling of the grain price so that stockpiles would be redirected to the urban population. She wrote to her husband, reassuring him that she had the crisis in hand and would govern proactively on his behalf:

> I will govern matters of state here in such a way that you will neither be troubled, nor damaged, and everything will be done for the good of the subjects. And when something is said or written about disorder, and you have not been advised of it by me, assume it is a lie since I allow not only officials, but any subject, to have the opportunity to speak to me whenever

---

[141] 20 June 1491, cited and translated in M. Bourne, *Francesco II Gonzaga: The Soldier-Prince As Patron* (Rome: Bulzoni, 2008), pp. 37–8.

[142] Last day of February 1495, in James, *A Renaissance Marriage*, p. 77, n. 18.

they want to, so nothing can happen without it being anticipated before any disorder follows.[143]

This cautious approach was key to Isabella's success in quelling public scepticism about such a young woman's ability to rule her husband's state in wartime.

In contrast to the detailed record of Isabella's efforts over three decades to preserve stable government in Mantua in a wartime climate, the political work of her sister-in-law Lucrezia Borgia as duchess of neighbouring Ferrara was substantially constrained by her many pregnancies, frequent illnesses, and early death. In 1497, Alfonso d'Este was already so incapacitated by the Great Pox, perceived by Italians as having been introduced and spread in Italy by the French invaders, that he was unable to attend the funeral of his first wife, Anna Sforza.[144] It is likely that Alfonso infected Lucrezia, since she enjoyed robust health before marrying him in 1502 but subsequently endured multiple miscarriages and declined physically in the years preceding her demise in 1519, at the age of thirty-nine.

Yet, in the last decade of her life, Lucrezia made important contributions to the Este war effort. Her rich dowry proved a vital asset in the 1509 Battle of the Polesella, a naval battle on the River Po in the War of the League of Cambrai, during which Ferrarese artillery destroyed the Venetian fleet moored on a tributary of the Po, within striking distance of Ferrara. By pawning her jewels, Lucrezia provided her husband with funds for powerful and innovative cannons, which were levelled at the enemy ships under cover of night and fired at first light, taking the Venetians by surprise.[145] This humiliating defeat profoundly undermined the republic's military confidence and marked the end of its hitherto aggressive expansion into the *terraferma*.[146]

Alfonso d'Este's heavy artillery was also decisive in delivering a French-imperial victory at the 1512 Battle of Ravenna.[147] However, the death of Gaston de Foix and severe loss of life among other nobles during the battle persuaded Louis XII to order his army to retreat to France. The king's ally, Emperor Maximilian I, also withdrew his troops from Italy and then promptly changed sides. Ferrara was thus left isolated as Julius II prepared to attack the duchy and reclaim it as the Church's territorial patrimony after successfully driving out the rulers of papal cities such as Ravenna, Faenza, and

---

[143] 30 June 1495, in James, *A Renaissance Marriage*, p. 87, n. 51.

[144] B. Zambotti, *Diario ferrarese dall'anno 1476 sino al 1504*, ed. G. Pardi (Modena: Zanichelli, 1934), pp. 276–7.

[145] On Lucrezia's financial acumen, see D. Y. Ghirardo, 'Lucrezia Borgia as entrepreneur', *Renaissance Quarterly*, 61.1 (2008), 53–91.

[146] Shaw and Mallet, *The Italian Wars,* pp. 88–93.

[147] Shaw and Mallet, *The Italian Wars*, pp. 107–8.

Bologna.[148] Lucrezia again came to the rescue. Pawning more of her jewellery, she paid for the building of a great ditch and embankments around Ferrara.[149] As well as providing funds for artillery and protective earthworks, Lucrezia oversaw other military preparations for the defence of Ferrara after Julius II lured Alfonso to Rome to negotiate a peace settlement, only to find himself arrested and imprisoned. Lucrezia organised the fortification of bastions close to state borders in a period that saw the papal army occupy nearby towns such as Carpi, Reggio, and Brescello. She also issued military orders on her husband's behalf.[150] On 27 August 1512, for example, she wrote to Badino da Pavia, the most important military captain in the Ferrarese army, ordering that anyone trying to pass the Bastion of the Zaniolo, a crucial crossing point on the Po River, should be arrested and sent immediately to her brother-in-law, Cardinal Ippolito d'Este, for interrogation.[151] Two days later, she sent a messenger to Mantua, begging another brother-in-law, Francesco Gonzaga, to supply men-at-arms for the Este war effort.[152] As flagbearer of the papal army, the marquis of Mantua was the leading commander of the opposite side. Yet, judging from the frequency with which the duchess' agents travelled back and forth between Ferrara and Gonzaga's palace in Mantua, Lucrezia must have cooperated closely and surreptitiously with Francesco to undermine Julius' campaign to overthrow the Este.[153]

Lucrezia also outwitted the pope's spies while Alfonso was imprisoned in Rome by communicating with her husband through an ingenious secret code, probably devised by her secretary, Pietro Antonio Acciaioli. The cipher, the key to which survives among Este papers in the State Archive of Modena, is unconventional. Instead of the usual system of replacing certain letters with encoded symbols, Lucrezia sent confidential updates to Alfonso about the war through seemingly innocuous references to their four-year-old son, Ercole II d'Este, or statements about her own state of health and that of other family members. For example, when she wrote 'the eldest boy is well', Alfonso was to understand that the French army

[148] Shaw and Mallet, *The Italian Wars*, pp. 106–9.

[149] See P. Cremonini, 'Missive ingannevoli e verità nascoste. Vero e verosimile svelati da un cifrario di Lucrezia Borgia d'Este conservato nell'archivio di stato di Modena', in Ghirardo (ed.), *Lucrezia Borgia Lettere 1494–1519* (Mantua: Direzione generale Archivi, Tre Lune Edizioni, 2020), pp. xvii–xxxi (p. xxvii).

[150] For another example of military management by an elite women see S. Bowd, 'Gender, war and the state: The military management of Alda Pio Gambara during the Italian Wars', in Bowd, Cockram, and Gagné (eds.), *Shadow Agents*, pp. 253–276.

[151] 27 August 1513, Ghirardo (ed.), *Lettere*, p. 478.

[152] 29 August 1512, Ghirardo (ed.), *Lettere*, p. 479.

[153] Many of Lucrezia's letters to Francesco Gonzaga from this period merely introduce her agents. They would deliver the message in person, so avoiding the danger that confidential information would be intercepted by spies. See Ghirardo (ed.), *Lettere*, pp. 470–1, 475–9.

was retreating towards the Alps. The phrase 'I am well' conveyed urgent danger and meant 'Come home as quickly as possible', while 'Master Sigismondo says he will recover' was code for 'Spanish forces have arrived in the Romagna'.[154] Alfonso finally escaped from Rome with the covert help of Fabrizio and Marco Antonio Colonna, who were grateful for the good treatment that Fabrizio had received while he had been held in Ferrara as a prisoner of war. It is likely that Lucrezia had overseen that friendly hospitality.[155]

Like Isabella d'Este, Lucrezia was highly aware of the importance of diplomatic gift giving. Her letters document the to and fro of seasonal produce between Ferrara and Mantua and requests for help to import food across state borders in periods when famine and shortages caused by the war threatened to provoke urban unrest. Gifts were also essential to keep foreign alliances alive. While Alfonso was at the French court in late 1518, Lucrezia sent perfumed cushions to the queen Claude de France, who responded with grateful thanks and a request for perfumed gloves. Lucrezia also organised a luxury gift for François I after Alfonso requested that the French king be sent a pair of beautiful shirts with perfumed collars finely embroidered with gold thread.[156]

Sisterly Diplomacy

By the time Lucrezia Borgia was assisting Alfonso to defeat his political enemies, her father, Alexander VI, and her brother, Cesare Borgia, were dead. She therefore did not face the dilemma of reconciling the dynastic interests of natal and marital kin. The relationship between Francesco Gonzaga and his sister Clara, however, was bedevilled by the marquis' expectation that she would always privilege his political needs over those of her Bourbon children. Clara assumed that her brother would recognise the superior status she had acquired through marriage to Count Gilbert of Montpensier Bourbon, cousin to Charles VIII. Although she adhered to conventional gendered rhetoric in acknowledging Francesco's authority as the patriarch, occasionally her letters reveal her identification with the greater power and prestige of her Bourbon relatives. We see this attitude in a letter sent to Francesco in the spring of 1494, which discusses Charles VIII's preparations for war and insistently urges her brother to declare himself a French ally without delay:

> The opinion and advice of his lordship and mine would be that Your Lordship should ally with His Sacred Majesty, the king, and certainly you can be sure that at present it is impossible to find among Christians a stronger or more secure alliance. So, I beg that you please ponder and consider how the other

---

[154] The cipher is published in Cremonini, 'Missive ingannevoli', pp. xxii–xxv.
[155] Cremonini, 'Missive ingannevoli', p. xxviii.　　[156] Ghirardo (ed.), *Lettere*, p. 23.

great lords of Italy have come willingly to declare their every support and
favour to his majesty. Your Lordship will, therefore, think well on this matter
and then communicate his opinion to the abovementioned my lord and to me,
and his lordship and I will then do more for you than for ourselves.[157]

Instead, Francesco ignored his sister's advice and fought with the anti-French
Italian League, formed hastily in the aftermath of Charles VIII's spectacular
victory in Naples.

Following her husband Gilbert's death in late 1495, after he was captured during
the retaking of Naples by the Aragonese, Clara found that her high status as a lady-
in-waiting to Anne de Bretagne was enhanced by her connection to a man regarded
in France as a war hero. Louis XII came to the throne in 1498 and married his
predecessor's widow. Thus Clara's position within Anne entourage became even
more important, especially after the new king embarked on his campaign to
conquer Milan. Clara expected her brother to remain steadfastly Francophile during
Louis XII's campaign to drive their Sforza relatives from power. However, in 1500,
Francesco covertly aided Lodovico Sforza's attempt to recover the duchy of Milan
from French control and permitted his brother, Giovanni Gonzaga, to fight Louis
XII's army as a Sforza ally, a move that infuriated Louis XII, who threatened to
attack Mantua and depose the marquis in retaliation.

Clara had to work very hard to stop this from happening. She and her eldest
children eventually persuaded the king to forgive Francesco's disloyalty and
Clara herself played a central role in briefing Francesco's envoys and securing
them a sympathetic hearing in Milan and at the royal court in France. On
21 November 1500, with the success of her campaign to placate Louis XII
within sight, Clara urged her brother 'to remain constant in your good intentions
and devotion towards this most holy lord king, who is a god on earth and a wise
man who keeps his promises'. Yet, in the early months of 1501, with the
immediate danger to his state averted, Francesco no longer sent his sister copies
of correspondence with Louis XII. Clara interpreted this neglect as evidence
that her brother was not duly appreciative of the extraordinary lengths to which
she had gone in defending him. In the letter of 4 May 1501, she expressed her
disapproval and disappointment:

> Before long, I hope to be with the king to pursue my own affairs. I will not try to
> raise your situation to avoid being mocked. In France, there is a well-known
> proverb that whoever wishes to remain within the limits of the rules of prudence
> and does not wish to risk being laughed at, or mocked, will never do, or try to
> speak in support of, something that is senseless, or lacks foundation. I want to

---

[157] Clara Gonzaga to Francesco Gonzaga, 25 April 1494, in James, 'Diplomacy of Clara Gonzaga',
p. 490, n. 12.

say just one thing. From my heart I exhort you to turn your mind to how you might sweeten the king's feelings towards you and try harder to serve him obediently and affectionately since, if we wish to speak frankly, he alone of all the lords of the world can dispense benefit and harm.[158]

Francesco took little long-term notice of his sister's angry letter, assuming, as he had always done, that he could make use of Clara's advocacy when he found himself in a tight diplomatic corner, but sideline her when it was expedient to do so.

Francesco's failure adequately to acknowledge the extent to which Clara's diplomacy contributed to his ability to survive politically was an inevitable consequence of his determination to maintain the illusion that he remained in firm control of his own political fate. He also took for granted that it was Clara's duty to acquiesce obediently to whatever the Gonzaga dynastic project required of her. Clara's letter of 4 May communicates her frustration at Francesco's failure to understand the complexities of her situation as intermediary between families with very different understandings of their place in the European hierarchy of power.

Asserting Women's Political Authority

Italy's princely consorts projected authority and social status, often in collaboration with artists and literary figures who produced works that proclaimed their magnificence and learning, but also through their own gift giving and letter writing.[159] We see this particularly clearly in the case of Isabella d'Este, who bolstered her authority by commissioning works of art that associated her with political virtues such as prudence, magnificence, and fortitude.[160] Isabella's self-fashioning is on display in a portrait medallion produced in 1498 by the sculptor and medallist Gian Cristoforo Romano (Figure 9). The lettering of her name in classical style and the hairstyle that evokes those of ancient Roman empresses communicate Isabella's concern to be perceived as having an illustrious dynastic pedigree and as steeped in ancient culture. The reverse features the zodiac sign of Sagittarius flying above a winged female victory, likely an allusion to the marchioness' fitness to exercise authority.[161] That political

---

[158] The letter is published in L. G. Pélissier, 'Les relations de François de Gonzague, marquis de Mantoue avec Ludovic Sforza et Louis XII, notes additionnelles et documents', *Annales de la Faculté de lettres de Bordeaux*, 15 (1893), 50–96 (91–2).

[159] On the broader chronological and social context of Italian women's letter writing, see M. Ray, *Writing Gender in Women's Letter Collections of the Italian Renaissance* (Toronto: Toronto University Press, 2009); D. Robin and L. Westwater (eds.), *Duchess and Hostage in Renaissance Naples: Letters and Orations, Ippolita Sforza* (Toronto: Iter Press 2017); S. G. Ross, *The Birth of Feminism: Woman As Intellect in Renaissance Italy and England* (Cambridge MA: Harvard University Press, 2009).

[160] James, 'Political image making'.

[161] See L. Syson, 'Reading faces: Gian Cristoforo Romano's medal of Isabella d'Este', in C. Mozzarelli, R. Oresko, and L. Venturi (eds.), *La corte di Mantova nell'età di Andrea Mantegna: 1450–1550* (Rome: Bulzoni, 1997), pp. 281–94.

(a)   (b)

Figure 9 a and b Gian Cristoforo Romano, Medal of Isabella d'Este, obverse and reverse, 1498; bronze, diameter 38 mm. Bequest of Anne D. Thomson, 1923, Metropolitan Museum of Art, New York, Accession Number 23.280.20

message seems to have been effectively understood by those who were presented with a medallion. The Gonzaga chancery secretary Jacopo d'Atri, for example, wrote to Isabella from Naples on 24 October 1507, relating that the arrival of one of the silver medals had caused a sensation at the Neapolitan court, those who examined it concluding that the profile image of Isabella 'indicated a great intelligence'.[162]

Isabella's desire to be portrayed as majestic and politically resolute but also learned is similarly evident in Leonardo da Vinci's profile portrait of her from 1500, completed while Leonardo was briefly in Mantua after fleeing war-torn Milan. Made in coloured chalks, the drawing, now in the Louvre Museum, has pricking holes that indicate that the portrait was copied multiple times, probably for distribution as diplomatic gifts. It is likely this process that weakened the sheet and led to the base of the drawing being cropped, perhaps even in Isabella's own day. One copy, made in Leonardo's workshop, reveals what was lost from the original (Figure 10). Isabella's hands rested on a ledge, with the index finger of her right hand pointing to a book that lies on the same shelf, reminding the viewer of Isabella's intellectual and literary interests.[163] Leonardo's drawing served the same function as the medallion – communicating Isabella's reputation as prudent

---

[162] A. Luzio, 'I ritratti d'Isabella d'Este', in *La Galleria dei Gonzaga venduta all'Inghilterra nel 1627–28* (Milan: Cogliati, 1913), pp. 183–238 (p. 194). On other avenues of self-fashioning, see S. Cockram, 'Isabella d'Este's sartorial politics', in E. Griffey (ed.), *Sartorial Politics in Early Modern Europe: Fashioning Women* (Amsterdam: Amsterdam University Press, 2019), pp. 35–56.

[163] F. Ames-Lewis, *Isabella and Leonardo: The Artistic Relationship between Isabella d'Este and Leonardo da Vinci* (New Haven, CT: Yale University Press, 2012), pp. 128–30.

Figure 10 After Leonardo da Vinci, Portrait of Isabella d'Este, 1467–1519; black chalk on paper, 629 mm x 484 mm. Bequeathed by Francis Douce, 1834, Ashmolean Museum, Oxford, Accession Number WA1863.617

and politically astute at a dangerous point in the Wars. Louis XII's defeat of Lodovico Sforza and the passing of the duchy of Milan into French hands in 1499 had brought a foreign power very close to the marquisate's borders. It was therefore imperative that the Gonzaga regime should be perceived as in capable hands.

Leonardo's portrait of Isabella was unusual in that it did not form part of a conjugal pair, as was the case with Raphael's portrait of her sister-in-law Elisabetta Gonzaga (Figure 8), which was meant to sit alongside a matching portrait of her spouse, Guidobaldo Montefeltro, completed by Raphael in 1508. Portraits of Isabella's daughter-in-law Margherita Paleologo and eldest daughter, Eleonora Gonzaga, painted by Titian and Giulio Romano respectively, were also conceived as complementing representations of their husbands in soldierly garb.[164] Isabella followed her mother's example in presenting herself visually as possessing the ability to rule on her own, something that was obliquely defended in literary works by male clients who defended the ability of both women to exercise political authority. The evolution of the pictorial cycle in Isabella's study from the idealisation of a political collaboration between dynastic spouses in Andrea Mantegna's

---

[164] See James, 'Political image making'.

Parnassus of 1497, to a more particular focus on herself, conveyed obliquely in Lorenzo Costa's *Coronation of a Lady* (1504–6), documents Isabella's ambition to be given greater leeway in decision-making, as an acknowledgement of her maturity and demonstrated political competence.[165] It was this aspiration that eventually caused friction with her husband.[166]

Francesco's collaboration with Isabella was in some senses more straightforward than that with his sister Clara because the couple was equally invested in passing on the marquisate to the next Gonzaga generation. However, Francesco's concern to be perceived as entirely in charge politically eventually provoked conflict in this relationship as well. The marquis was captured and imprisoned in Venice for almost an entire year in August 1509 as a retrospective punishment for his secret courting of Charles VIII between 1495 and 1497 while he was receiving a Venetian salary as a military captain of the Italian League. Isabella had suddenly to exercise authority entirely without her husband's oversight since Francesco was kept incommunicado. Louis XII and Emperor Maximilian I each tried to install their representatives at the head of government in Mantua on the grounds that it was too risky to have a woman in charge. They also made separate demands that Isabella allow her ten-year old son to be held at their court as a hostage, in return for help in negotiating Francesco's freedom from captivity. In return for help in negotiating Francesco's freedom from captivity. Isabella refused both demands, agreeing, after many months of negotiation, to entrust Federico to Pope Julius II, knowing that the boy would be well cared for and would remain in Italy.[167]

Isabella's astute diplomacy and attentive stewardship of the Gonzaga regime during Francesco's humiliating imprisonment showcased her abilities to rule alone. The 1512 Congress of Mantua compounded the delicate politics of the couple's collaboration. This meeting of the Holy League, of which the pope was a member, was convened to divide the spoils of war following the collapse of Louis XII's military campaign in northern Italy. Isabella had no official role during the Congress and, as a woman, could not attend its sessions. However, she worked effectively behind the scenes to prevent the Holy League from obeying Pope Julius II's demand that its army should immediately attack Ferrara. An eyewitness wrote of Isabella's first encounter with the Spanish viceroy of Naples, Ramón de Cardona, describing how cleverly she took advantage of Mantua's artistic heritage and the prestige associated with her own collections of antiquities and paintings by Andrea

---

[165] S. Campbell, *The Cabinet of Eros: Renaissance Mythological Painting and the Studiolo of Isabella d'Este* (New Haven, CT: Yale University Press, 2004).

[166] See James, *A Renaissance Marriage*, pp. 134–83.

[167] See A. Luzio, 'Federico Gonzaga ostaggio alla corte di Giulio II', *Archivio della Società Romana di Storia Patria*, 9 (1886), 509–82.

Mantegna, Lorenzo Costa, and Pietro Perugino to convince the foreign visit-
ors to take her seriously as a woman of diplomatic consequence. 'Everyone
went into the painted room [Andrea Mantegna's *Camera degli sposi*] and,
after remaining there talking for some time, the gentlemen of the viceroy went
to see all the rooms of Milady, which they praised to the skies, the company
claiming that they had never seen such refined spaces, not witnessed such
refined decorations.'[168] By the end of the Congress, Isabella was able to assure
her brother Cardinal Ippolito d'Este that she had convinced the Holy League's
delegates to defer the overthrow of the Este regime until other pressing
matters, such as the restoration of Sforza rule in Milan, had been implemented.
Crucially, Isabella delayed the departure from Mantua of Ramón de Cardona
by engineering a dalliance between the Spanish viceroy and one of her most
beautiful ladies-in-waiting. The temporary reprieve she achieved for her
brothers proved pivotal since Julius II died several months later in early
1513, removing the threat to Ferrara.

However, Isabella's high diplomatic profile during the Congress was challenging for her husband, whose formerly robust health was progressively being
destroyed by the debilitating effects of the Great Pox. Between the Congress
and his premature death in early 1519, Francesco clung on to remnants of the
hyper-masculine image he had previously projected by recourse to a more
aggressively authoritarian persona. He also distanced himself from the earlier
political collaborations with his wife. Isabella therefore remained for lengthy
periods at the court of her inexperienced nephew Massimiliano Sforza, the
newly installed Duke of Milan, and travelled to Rome, where she lobbied
Pope Leo X for various political favours for Gonzaga and Este relatives.[169] It
seems that her significant diplomatic roles during the early crises generated in
northern Italy by the Wars eroded her preparedness to be merely a passive
political instrument.

Isabella's political work went beyond that of her mother in Ferrara during the
1480s and, by her middle years, the marchioness' name and her reputation as
a political actor were well known in the courts of France and Spain.
Noblewomen there and in Italy emulated her fashions and were curious to
know about her latest style inventions.[170] She was also seen by contemporaries
as a remarkably successful cultural patron. The artworks she commissioned

---

[168]   Amico della Torre to Federico Gonzaga, 13 August 1512, in Luzio, 'Isabella d'Este di fronte
a Giulio II', 18 (1912), p. 114.

[169]   James, *A Renaissance Marriage*, pp. 159–83.

[170]   See A. Luzio and R. Renier, 'Il lusso di Isabella d'Este, Marchesa di Mantova', *Nuova
Antologia*, s. 4, 63 (1896), 441–69; Y. C. Croizat, '"Living dolls": François Ier dresses his
women', *Renaissance Quarterly*, 60.1 (2007), 94–130.

from some of Italy's most accomplished masters, her collection of precious antiquities, and her discerning patronage of music and literature all contributed to her renown.

In Summary

In Italian settings, where political survival relied on the combined efforts of female as well as male members of ruling families, there were frequent opportunities for a pragmatic bending of the rules governing elite female access to the political sphere, especially in a time of war. The administrative and diplomatic competence of individuals such as Clara Gonzaga and Isabella d'Este proved crucial to the Gonzaga regime in the early years of the sixteenth century when there was a high risk that Mantua would become French territory. The women's political abilities were recognised by ambassadors, foreign monarchs, and members of their own courts. This recognition gave both women the confidence to push back against the Gonzaga patriarch's assumption that their personal honour should be subsumed by his. Family correspondence reveals that while the women observed the rhetoric of obedience required of their sex, they also vigorously defended their ability to balance loyalties to natal and marital kin and to do so on their own terms. Lucrezia Borgia emerges from her letters as political capable and utterly loyal to her Este relatives, in stark contradiction to the poisonous myths about her sexual depravity and murderous past that were created and weaponised by enemies of her father and brother during the papacy of Alexander VI. All three women examined in this section made important administrative, diplomatic, and financial contributions to the ability of their menfolk to retain power in states threatened by war on their very doorstep.

Conclusion

This Element has argued that theoretical engagement with gender identity, ideologies, and relations can deliver significant new insights about the Italian Wars. Whether in empires, monarchies, or the Italian principalities, male rulers frequently made these conflicts about themselves as individuals. Their personal engagement in forms of power that required them to assert their physical prowess and courage, virile sexuality, and reproductive capabilities, often using women's bodies to make these claims, created opportunities for female relatives to perform authority on their behalf, especially as regents and as governors. In doing so, they operated within gender ideologies as proxies for men. The Wars were predicated on the ability of male leaders to rely on female family members providing dynastic service. Early modern men knew that the

Wars depended on women's participation and contribution; our histories need to take account of that crucial work.

In all the various contexts examined here, elite women were expected to participate in the diplomatic work of (sometimes both) their natal and marital families and many were crucially involved in the war-mongering and peace-making associated with the conflicts. The women featured in the preceding sections acknowledged (at least rhetorically) their subordinate place in the dynastic pecking order. Their letters certainly offer insights into some of the challenges they faced but, importantly, they also provide evidence of the capacity to express dissent to, or about, the patriarch in carefully couched forms and to exercise agency in certain circumstances.

Looking through the lens of gender and at the activities of women also prompts a reconsideration of early modern war, where its activities took place, and what its actions consisted of, extending narrow definitions of war beyond military actions and manoeuvres. Although female protagonists have been our primary focus, this broader approach to war permits a reconfiguration of our understanding of how men too deployed power well beyond direct military action or during official diplomatic engagements. Key aspects of the conflict played out not on the battlefield, but rather in winning the hearts and minds of allies and of subjects terrified by the prospect that the conflicts would bring destruction and death to their towns and cities. The campaigns of persuasion waged through cultural forms of politics, including a wide range of media presentations, especially artistic endeavours, gave elite women important roles in producing men's power. They furthermore provided women with opportunities to manipulate their own public image and associate themselves with attributes that would bolster their legitimacy in similar ways to male leaders. Many of their cultural productions placed emphasis on advancing themselves as women of influence, authority, or power, showing (for better or worse) that they too could be protagonists of war as well as peacemakers.

Bibliography

Primary Sources

Anne of France, *Lessons for My Daughter*, trans. and ed. S. L. Janson (Cambridge: D. S. Brewer, 2012).

Baschet, A., *La diplomatie vénitienne: Les princes de l'Europe au XVIe siècle* (Paris: Plon, 1862).

Bauer, W., and R. Lacroix (eds.), *Die Korrespondenz Ferdinands I*, 4 vols. (Vienna: Adolf Holzhausen, 1912–38).

Bergh, L. P. van den, *Correspondance de Marguerite d'Autriche, gouvernante des Pays-Bas, avec ses amis, sur les affaires des Pays-Bas de 1506–1528*, 2 vols. (Leiden: S. et J. Luchtmans, 1845–7).

Boom, G. de (ed.), *Correspondance de Marguerite d'Autriche et de ses ambassadeurs à la cour de France concernant l'exécution du traité de Cambrai, 1529–1530* (Brussels: Maurice Lamertin, 1935).

Bradford, W. (ed.), *Correspondence of the Emperor Charles V and His Ambassadors at the Courts of England and France from the Original Letters in the Imperial Family Archives at Vienna with a Connecting Narrative and Biographical Notes of the Emperor and of Some of the Most Distinguished Officers of His Army and Household together with the Emperor's Itinerary from 1519–1551* (London: R. Bentley, 1850).

Brewer, J. S. (ed.), *Letters and Papers, Foreign and Domestic, Henry VIII*, 12 vols. (London: Her Majesty's Stationery Office, 1862–1910), vol. III (1867): '1519–1523'. *British History Online*. www.british-history.ac.uk/letters-papers-hen8/vol3.

Brown, R. (ed.), *Calendar of State Papers relating to English Affairs in the Archives of Venice 1509–1519*, 38 vols. (London: Her Majesty's Stationery Office, 1864–1947), vol. II (1867): '1509–1519'. *British History Online*. www.british-history.ac.uk/cal-state-papers/venice/vol2.

Cerretani, B., *Ricordi*, ed. G. Berti (Florence: Olschki, 1993).

Champollion-Figeac, A. (ed.), *Poésies, et correspondance intime du roi avec Diane de Poitiers et plusieurs autres dames de la cour du roi François Ier, de Louise de Savoie, duchesse d'Angoulême, de Marguerite, reine de Navarre* (Geneva: Slatkine, 1847, 1970).

Collett, B., *A Long and Troubled Pilgrimage: The Correspondence of Marguerite d'Angoulême and Vittoria Colonna, 1540–1545* (Princeton, NJ: Princeton Theological Seminary, 2000).

Chazaud, M. A. (ed.), *Les enseignements d'Anne de France, duchesse de Bourbonnois et d'Auvergne, à sa fille Susanne de Bourbon* (Moulins: Desrosiers, 1878).

Fernández Álvarez, M. (ed.), *Corpus Documental de Carlos V*, 5 vols. (Salamanca: Ediciones Universidad de Salamanca, 1973–81).

Gairdner, J. (ed.), *Letters and Papers, Foreign and Domestic, Henry VIII*, 12 vols. (London, 1862–1910), vol. VI (1882): '1533'. *British History Online.* www.british-history.ac.uk/letters-papers-hen8/vol6.

Ghirardo, D. Y. (ed.), *Lucrezia Borgia Lettere 1494–1519* (Mantua: Direzione generale Archivi, Tre Lune Edizioni, 2020).

Gorter-van Royen, L. V. G., and J.-P. Hoyois (eds.), *Correspondance de Marie de Hongrie avec Charles Quint et Nicolas de Granvelle*, 2 vols. (Turnhout: Brepols, 2009–18).

Guasti, C., *Scritti storici* (Prato: Stefano-Belli, 1894).

Hatvani, M. (ed.), *Magyar Történelmi okmánytár a Brusseli orszagos levéltárból és a burgundi könyvtárbol*, 4 vols. (Pest: Monumenta hungarica historica, 1857–8).

'Inventari der Pressburgishn clainater', *Jahrbuch der Kunsthistorischen Sammlungen des Allerhöchsten Kaiserhauses*, 3 (1885), cxli–ii, nos. 3005–7.

'König Ferdinand I. schreibt wegen der Pressburger Kleinodien an der Räthe der neiderösterreichischen Raitkammer', *Jahrbuch der Kunsthistorischen Sammlungen des Allerhöchsten Kaiserhauses*, 3 (1885), cxl, no. 3003.

Lambert, Abbé C.-F. (ed.), 'Journal de Louise de Savoie, duchesse d'Angoulesme, d'Anjou et de Valois, mère du grand roi François premier', in M. Petitot et al. (eds.), *Collection complète des mémoires relatifs à l'histoire de France*, 131 vols. (Paris: Foucault, 1819–29), vol. XVI (1826), pp. 383–408.

Landucci, L., *Diario fiorentino dal 1450 al 1516*, ed. Iodoco del Badia (Florence: Studio Biblos, 1969).

Le Glay, A.-J.-G. (ed.), *Correspondance de l'empereur Maximilien Ier et de Marguerite d'Autriche, sa fille, gouvernante des Pays Bas, de 1507–1519*, 2 vols. (Paris: J. Renouard et Cie, 1839).

Le Glay, A.-J.-G. (ed.), *Négociations diplomatiques entre la France et l'Autriche durant les trente premières années du XVIe siècle*, 2 vols. (Paris: Imprimerie royale, 1845).

Macchiavelli, N., *The Prince*, trans. G. Bull (London: Penguin Books, 2004).

Margaret of Navarre, *The Heptameron of the Tales of Margaret, Queen of Navarre*, 5 vols. (London: Gibbings and Company [1898]).

Marguerite de Navarre, *The Heptameron*, trans. P. A. Chilton (London: Penguin, 1984, 2004).

Mary of Hungary, Testament 3 December 1555, *Jahrbuch der Kunsthistorischen Sammlungen des Allerhöchsten Kaiserhauses*, 11 (1890), lxvii, no. 6477.

Mercati, A., *Lettere di Elisabetta e di Leonora Gonzaga a Francesco Maria della Rovere* (Mantua: Reale Accademia Virgiliana di Mantova, 1941).

Modesti, J., 'Il miserando sacco dato alla terra di Prato dagli Spagnoli l'anno 1512', *Archivio Storico Italiano*, 1 (1842), 233–51.

Quinsonas, E. de, *Matériaux pour server à l'histoire de Marguerite d'Autriche*, 3 vols. (Paris: Delaroque Frères, 1809).

Robin, D., and L. Westwater (eds.), *Duchess and Hostage in Renaissance Naples: Letters and Orations, Ippolita Sforza* (Toronto: Iter Press, 2017).

Romei, D. (ed.), *Scritti di Pietro Aretino nel codice Marciano IT.XI 66 (=6730)* (Florence: F. Cesati, 1987).

Spielman, D. C., and C. Thomas, 'Quellen zur Jugend Erzherzog Ferdinands I. in Spanien: Bisher unbekannte Briefe Karls V. an seinen Bruder (1514–1517)', *Mitteilungen des Österreichischen Staatsarchiv*, 37 (1984), 1–34.

Tommaseo, N. (ed.), *Relations des ambassadeurs vénitiens sur les affaires de France au XVIe siècle*, 2 vols. (Paris: Imprimerie royale, 1838).

Viaud, A. (ed.), *Lettres des souverains portugais à Charles-Quint et à l'Impératrice (1528–1532)* (Lisbon: Centre Culturel Calouste Gulbenkian, 1994).

Weiss, C. (ed.), *Papiers d'Etat du Cardinal de Granvelle*, 9 vols. (Paris: Imprimerie nationale, 1841–52).

Zambotti, B., *Diario ferrarese dall'anno 1476 sino al 1504*, ed. G. Pardi (Modena: Zanichelli, 1934).

Secondary Sources

Abulafia, D., *The French Descent into Italy, 1494–5: Antecedents and Effects* (Aldershot: Ashgate, 1995).

Adams, T., and C. Adams, *The Creation of the French Royal Mistress: From Agnès Sorel to Madame Du Barry* (University Park: Pennsylvania State University Press, 2020).

Akkerman, N., and B. Houben (eds.), *The Politics of Female Households: Ladies-in-Waiting across Early Modern Europe* (Leiden: Brill, 2014).

Alvar Ezquerra, A., *La Emperatriz* (Madrid: La Esfera de los Libros, 2012).

Ames-Lewis, F., *Isabella and Leonardo: The Artistic Relationship between Isabella d'Este and Leonardo da Vinci* (New Haven, CT: Yale University Press, 2012).

Andersson, C., 'Harlots and camp followers: Swiss Renaissance drawings of young women circa 1520', in E. S. Cohen and M. Reeves (eds.), *The Youth of Early Modern Women* (Amsterdam: Amsterdam University Press, 2018), pp. 117–34.

Attreed, L., 'Gender, patronage, and diplomacy in the early career of Margaret of Austria (1480–1530)', *Mediterranean Studies*, 20.1 (2012), 3–27.

Barthe, P., *French Encounters with the Ottomans, 1510–1560* (London: Routledge, 2016).

Beer, M., D. Diamanti, and C. Ivaldi (eds.), *Guerre in ottava rima*, 4 vols. (Modena: Edizioni Panini, 1989), vol. II: 'Guerre d'Italia (1483–1527)'.

Bendall, S. A., 'Adorning masculinities? The commissioning and wearing of hat badges during the Habsburg–Valois Italian Wars', *Sixteenth Century Journal*, 52.3 (2021), 539–70.

Bendall, S. A., 'Female personifications and masculine forms: Gender, armour and allegory in the Habsburg–Valois conflicts of sixteenth-century Europe', *Gender & History*, 35.1 (2023), 42–67.

Bokody, P., 'Images of wartime sexual violence in the chronicles of Giovanni Villani and Giovanni Sercambi', *Renaissance Studies*, 36.4 (2021), 565–89.

Boom, G. de, *Archiduchesse Éléonore, reine de France; soeur de Charles Quint* (Brussels: Le Cri, 1943).

Bourne, M., *Francesco II Gonzaga: The Soldier-Prince As Patron* (Rome: Bulzoni, 2008).

Bourne, M., 'Mail humour and male sociability: Sexual innuendo in the epistolary domain of Francesco II Gonzaga', in S. F. Matthews-Grieco (ed.), *Erotic Cultures of Renaissance Italy* (Aldershot: Ashgate, 2010), pp. 199–221.

Bowd, S. D., *Renaissance Mass Murder: Civilians and Soldiers during the Italian Wars* (Oxford: Oxford University Press, 2018).

Bowd, S., S. Cockram, and J. Gagné (eds.), *Shadow Agents of Renaissance War: Suffering, Supporting, and Supplying Conflict in Italy and Beyond* (Amsterdam: Amsterdam University Press, 2023).

Brioist, P., L. Fagnart, and C. Michon (eds.), *Louise de Savoie (1476–1531)* (Tours: Presses universitaires François-Rabelais, 2015).

Broomhall, S., 'Alter egos: Mediterranean agents negotiating identity at the dawn of the Franco–Ottoman alliance', in Z. E. Rohr and J. W. Spangler (eds.), *Significant Others: Aspects of Deviance and Difference in Premodern Europe* (London: Routledge, 2021), pp. 81–109.

Broomhall, S., 'Corresponding romances: Henri II and the last campaigns of the Italian Wars', in S. Downes, A. Lynch, and K. O'Loughlin (eds.), *Writing War in Britain and France, 1370–1854: A History of Emotions* (London: Routledge, 2018), pp. 107–25.

Broomhall, S. (ed.), *Women and Power at the French Court, 1483–1563* (Amsterdam: Amsterdam University Press, 2018).

Broomhall, S., and J. Van Gent, *Dynastic Colonialism: Gender, Materiality and the Early Modern House of Orange-Nassau* (London: Routledge, 2016).

Broomhall, S., and J. Van Gent, *Gender, Power and Identity in the Early Modern House of Orange-Nassau* (London: Routledge, 2016).

Brown, C. J. (ed.), *The Cultural and Political Legacy of Anne de Bretagne: Negotiating Convention in Books and Documents* (Woodbridge: Boydell and Brewer, 2010).

Burckhardt, J., *Die Kultur der Renaissance in Italien* (Vienna: Phaidon, 1860).

Campbell, S., *The Cabinet of Eros: Renaissance Mythological Painting and the Studiolo of Isabella d'Este* (New Haven, CT: Yale University Press, 2004).

Champollion-Figeac, A., *Captivité du roi François Ier* (Paris: Imprimerie royale, 1847).

Cholakian, P., *Rape and Writing in the Heptaméron of Marguerite de Navarre* (Carbondale: Southern Illinois University Press, 1991).

Cockram, S., *Isabella d'Este and Francesco Gonzaga: Power Sharing at the Renaissance Court* (Farnham: Ashgate 2013).

Cockram, S., 'Isabella d'Este's sartorial politics', in E. Griffey (ed.), *Sartorial Politics in Early Modern Europe: Fashioning Women* (Amsterdam: Amsterdam University Press, 2019), pp. 35–56.

Crawford, P., 'Women's published writings 1600–1700', in M. Prior (ed.), *Women in English Society, 1500–1800* (London: Routledge, 1985), pp. 211–31.

Cremonini, P., 'Missive ingannevoli e verità nascoste: Vero e verosimile svelati da un cifrario di Lucrezia Borgia d'Este conservato nell'archivio di stato di Modena', in D. Ghirardo (ed.), *Lucrezia Borgia Lettere 1494–1519* (Mantua: Direzione generale Archivi, Tre Lune Edizioni, 2020), pp. xvii–xxxi.

Croizat, Y. C., '"Living dolls": François Ier dresses his women', *Renaissance Quarterly*, 60.1 (2007), 94–130.

Cruz, A. J., and M. Galli Stampino (eds.), *Early Modern Habsburg Women: Transnational Contexts, Cultural Conflicts, Dynastic Continuities* (London: Routledge, 2013).

Daybell, J., and S. Norrhem (eds.), *Gender and Political Culture in Early Modern Europe* (London: Routledge, 2017).

Dialeti, A., 'Defending women, negotiating masculinity in early modern Italy', *Historical Journal*, 54.1 (2011), 1–23.

Doyle, D. R., 'The sinews of Habsburg governance in the sixteenth century: Mary of Hungary and political patronage', *Sixteenth Century Journal*, 31.2 (2000), 349–60.

Dumont, J., L. Fagnart, N. Le Roux, and P.-G. Girault (eds.), *Les Paix des Dames, 1529: Diplomatie, genre et symbolique du pouvoir à la Renaissance* (Tours: Presses universitaires François-Rabelais, 2021).

Dupont-Pierrart, N., *Claire de Gonzague Comtesse de Bourbon-Montpensier (1464–1503): Une princesse italienne à la cour de France* (Lille: Septentrion, 2017).

Earenfight, T., 'Without the persona of the prince: Kings, queens, and the idea of monarchy in late medieval Europe', *Gender & History*, 19.1 (2007), 1–21.

Eichberger, D., 'The culture of gifts: A courtly phenomenon from a female perspective', in D. Eichberger (ed.), *Women of Distinction: Margaret of York and Margaret of Austria* (Turnhout: Brepols, 2005), pp. 286–95.

Eichberger, D., 'Margaret of Austria's portrait collection: Female patronage in the light of dynastic ambitions and artistic quality', *Renaissance Studies*, 10.2 (1996), 259–79.

Eichberger, D., and L. Beaven, 'Family members and political allies: The portrait collection of Margaret of Austria', *Art Bulletin*, 77.2 (1995), 225–48.

Fagel, R., 'Don Fernando en Flandes (1518–1521): Un príncipe sin tierra', in A. Alvar and F. Edelmayer (eds.), *Fernando I, 1503–1564: Socialización, vida privada y actividad pública de un Emperador del renacimiento* (Madrid: Sociedad Estatal de Conmemoraciones Culturales, 2004), pp. 253–71.

Feci, S., 'Signore di curia: Rapporti di potere ed esperienze di governo nella Roma papale (metà XV–metà XVI secolo)', in L. Arcangeli and S. Peyronel (eds.), *Donne di potere nel Rinascimento* (Rome: Viella, 2008), pp. 195–222.

Federinov, B., and G. Docquier (eds.), *Marie de Hongrie: Politique et culture sous la renaissance aux Pays-Bas. Actes du Colloque tenu au Musée royal de Mariemont les 11 et 12 novembre 2005* (Mariemont: Collections monographies du Musée royal de Mariemont, 2008).

Ferguson, G., and M. B. McKinley, 'The *Heptaméron*: Word, spirit, world', in G. Ferguson and M. B. McKinley (eds.), *A Companion to Marguerite de Navarre* (Leiden: Brill, 2013), pp. 323–71.

Fichtner, P. S., 'Dynastic marriage in sixteenth-century Habsburg diplomacy and statecraft: An interdisciplinary approach', *American Historical Review*, 81.2 (1976), 243–65.

Fisher, S., 'Queens consort, gender and diplomacy: Catherine of Aragon, Claude of France and the Field of Cloth of Gold', *Gender & History* 35.2 (2022), 387–407.

Fletcher, C., 'The Ladies' Peace revisited: Gender, counsel and diplomacy', in H. Matheson-Pollack, J. Paul, and C. Fletcher (eds.), *Queenship and Counsel in Early Modern Europe* (Basingstoke: Palgrave, 2018), pp. 111–33.

Fornaciari, A., R. Gaeta, S. Minozzi, and V. Giuffra, 'Syphilis in Maria Salviati (1499–1543), wife of Giovanni de' Medici of the Black Bands', *Emerging Infectious Diseases*, 26.6 (2020), 1274–82.

Fuchs, M., and O. Réthelyi (eds.), *Maria von Ungarn (1505–1558): Eine Renaissancefürstin* (Muenster: Achendorff, 2007).

Gachard, L. P. (ed.), *Retraite et mort de Charles-Quint au monastère de Yuste*, 3 vols. (Brussels: M. Hayez, 1854–5).

Gagné, J., 'Collecting women: Three French kings and manuscripts of empire in the Italian Wars', *I Tatti Studies in the Italian Renaissance*, 20.1 (2017), 127–84.

Gagné, J., *Milan Undone: Contested Sovereignties in the Italian Wars* (Cambridge, MA: Harvard University Press, 2021).

Geevers, L., 'The Danish Habsburgs: Hans, Dorothea and Christina of Denmark as part of the Habsburg dynasty', in E. Bodensten, K. Brilkman, D. L. Heidenblad, and H. Sanders (eds.), *Nordens Historiker: En vänbok till Harald Gustafsson* (Lund: Historiska institutionen, Lunds Universitet, 2018), pp. 273–86.

Geevers, L., and M. Marini (eds.), *Dynastic Identity in Early Modern Europe: Rulers, Aristocrats and the Formation of Identities* (London: Routledge, 2016).

Ghirardo, D. Y., 'Lucrezia Borgia as entrepreneur', *Renaissance Quarterly*, 61.1 (2008), 53–91.

Gonzaga, M., *Imperatriz Isabel de Portugal* (Lisbon: Bertrand Editora, 2012).

Gorter-van Royen, L. V. G., *Maria van Hongarije, regentes der Nederlanden: Een politieke analyse op basis van haar regentschapsordonnaties en haar corespondentie met Karel V* (Leiden: Hilversum, 1995).

Gschwend, A. J., '*Ma meilleur soeur*: Leonor of Austria, queen of Portugal and France', in F. Checa Cremades (ed.), *Los Inventarios de Carlos V y la Familia Imperial*, 3 vols. (Madrid: Fernando Villaverde, 2010), vol. III, pp. 2569–92.

Güttner-Sporzyński, D. von, 'Contextualising the marriage of Bona Sforza to Sigismund I of Poland: Maximilian I's diplomacy in Italy and Central Europe', *Folia Historica Cracoviensia*, 2 (2021), 69–90.

Güttner-Sporzyński, D. von, 'Daughter, mother, widow: The making of the identities of Isabella d'Aragona', *Gender & History*, early view (2023). https://doi.org/10.1111/1468-0424.12683.

Hackenbroch, Y., *Enseignes: Renaissance Hat Jewels* (Florence: Studio per Edizioni Scelte, 1996).

Hackenbroch, Y., 'Some portraits of Charles V', *Metropolitan Museum of Art Bulletin*, 27.6 (1969), 323–32.

Hauser, H., 'Le *Journal* de Louise de Savoie', *Revue historique*, 86 (1904), 280–303.

Hill, H. (ed.), *Architecture and the Politics of Gender in Early Modern Europe* (Farnham: Ashgate, 2003).

Hurlburt, H. S., *The Dogaressa of Venice, 1200–1500: Wife and Icon* (Houndsmills: Palgrave Macmillan, 2006).

Iongh, J. de (ed.), *Margaret of Austria: Regent of the Netherlands* (New York: W. W. Norton, 1953).

Iongh, J. de, *Mary of Hungary: Second Regent of the Netherlands*, trans. M. D. Herter Norton (New York: W. W. Norton, 1958).

Isom-Verhaaren, I., *Allies with the Infidel: The Ottoman and French Alliance in the Sixteenth Century* (London: Bloomsbury, 2013).

James, C., 'The diplomacy of Clara Gonzaga, countess of Montpensier-Bourbon: Gendered perspectives of family duty, honour and female agency', *Renaissance Studies*, 35.3 (2020), 486–502.

James, C., 'Florence and Ferrara: Dynastic marriage and politics', in R. Black and J. E. Law (eds.), *The Medici: Citizens and Masters* (Florence: Villa I Tatti, Harvard University Center for Italian Renaissance Studies, 2015), pp. 365–78.

James, C., 'Political image making in portraits of Isabella d'Este', *Gender & History*, 35.1 (2023), 20–41.

James, C., *A Renaissance Marriage: The Political and Personal Alliance of Isabella d'Este and Francesco, 1490–1519* (Oxford: Oxford University Press, 2020).

Jiménez Zamora, I., 'La actuación política de la Emperatriz Isabel (1528–1538)', *Espacio, tiempo y forma*, serie IV: Historia Moderna 29 (2016), 163–85.

Jiménez Zamora, I., 'La Emperatriz Isabel de Portugal y el Gobierno de la Monarquía Hispánica en tiempos de Carlos V (1526–1539)', unpublished PhD thesis, Universidad Nacional de Educación a Distancia (2015).

Kaplan, P. H. D., 'Giorgione's assault: War and rape in Renaissance Venice', in C. Baskins and L. Rosenthal (eds.), *Early Modern Visual Allegory: Embodying Meaning* (Aldershot: Ashgate, 2007), pp. 77–90.

Knecht, R. J., 'Eléonore d'Autriche (1498–1558)', in C. Michon (ed.), *Les Conseillers de François Ier* (Rennes: Presses universitaires de Rennes, 2011), pp. 401–14. https://books.openedition.org/pur/120045?lang=en.

Koenigsberger, H. G., *Monarchies, States Generals and Parliaments: The Netherlands in the Fifteenth and Sixteenth Centuries* (Cambridge: Cambridge University Press, 2001).

Konstam, A., *Pavia 1525: The Climax of the Italian Wars* (Oxford: Osprey, 1996).

Long, K. (ed.), *High Anxiety: Masculinity in Crisis in Early Modern France* (Kirksville, MO: Truman State University Press, 2002).

Luzio, A., 'Federico Gonzaga ostaggio alla corte di Giulio II', *Archivio della Società Romana di Storia Patria*, 9 (1886), 509–82.

Luzio, A., *La Galleria dei Gonzaga venduta all'Inghilterra nel 1627–28* (Milan: Cogliati, 1913).

Luzio, A., *La Galleria dei Gonzaga venduta all'Inghilterra nel 1627–28* (Milan: Cogliati, 1913).

Luzio, A., 'Isabella d'Este di fronte a Giulio II negli ultimi tre anni del suo pontificato', *Archivio storico lombardo*, 17 (1912), 245–334, and 18 (1912), 55–144 and 393–456.

Luzio, A., and R. Renier, 'Il lusso di Isabella d'Este, Marchesa di Mantova', *Nuova Antologia*, s. 4, 63 (1896), 441–69.

Luzio, A., and R. Renier, *Mantova e Urbino: Isabella d'Este ed Elisabetta Gonzaga nelle relazioni familiari e nelle vicende politiche* (Turin: Roux, 1893).

MacDonald, D., 'Collecting a new world: The ethnographic collections of Margaret of Austria', *Sixteenth Century Journal*, 33.3 (2002), 649–63.

Mallett, M., 'The transformation of war, 1494–1530', in C. Shaw (ed.), *Italy and the European Powers: The Impact of War, 1500–1530* (Leiden: Brill, 2006), pp. 3–21.

Mansfield, L., 'The art of conjugal discord: A satirical double portrait of Francis I and Eleanor of Austria, c. 1530–1535', in P. Sherlock and M. Cassidy-Welch (eds.), *Practices of Gender in Late Medieval and Early Modern Europe* (Turnhout: Brepols, 2008), 117–35.

Mansfield, L., *Representations of Renaissance Monarchy: Francis I and the Image-Makers* (Manchester: Manchester University Press, 2016).

Marzahl, P., 'Communication and control in the political system of Emperor Charles V: The first regency of Empress Isabella', in W. Blockman and N. Mout (eds.), *The World of Emperor Charles V* (Amsterdam: Royal Netherlands Academy of Arts and Sciences, 2004), pp. 83–96.

Mazarío Coleto, M. del C., *Isabel de Portugal, Emperatriz y Reina de España* (Madrid: Escuela de Historia Moderna, 1951).

Michelet, J., *Histoire de France au seizième siècle* (Paris: Chamerot, 1855).

Milligan, G., *Moral Combat: Women, Gender, and War in Italian Renaissance Literature* (Toronto: University of Toronto Press, 2018).

O'Leary, J., *Elite Women As Diplomatic Agents in Italy and Hungary, 1470–1510* (Leeds: ARC Humanities Press, 2022).

O'Leary, J., 'Politics, pedagogy, and praise: Three literary texts dedicated to Eleonora d'Aragona', *I Tatti Studies in the Italian Renaissance*, 19.2 (2016), 285–307.

Parker, G., *Emperor: A New Life of Charles V* (New Haven, CT: Yale University Press, 2019).

Patrouch, J. F., '"Bella gerant alli": Laodamia's sisters, Habsburg brides. Leaving home for the sake of the house', in A. J. Cruz and M. Galli Stampino (eds.), *Early Modern Habsburg Women: Transnational Contexts, Cultural Conflicts, Dynastic Continuities* (Farnham: Ashgate, 2013), pp. 25–40.

Pearson, A. (ed.), *Women and Portraits in Early Modern Europe: Gender, Agency, Identity* (London: Routledge, 2016).

Peebles, K. D., and G. Scarlatta (eds.), *Representing the Life and Legacy of Renée de France: From* Fille de France *to Dowager Duchess* (Cham: Springer, 2021).

Pélissier, L. G., 'Les relations de François de Gonzague, marquis de Mantoue avec Ludovic Sforza et Louis XII, notes additionnelles et documents', *Annales de la Faculté de lettres de Bordeaux*, 15 (1893), 50–96.

Pellegrini, M., *Le guerre d'Italia 1494–1530* (Bologna: il Mulino, 2009).

Perez, N. G. (ed.), *Mary of Hungary, Renaissance Patron and Collector: Gender, Art and Culture* (Turnhout: Brepols, 2020).

Pesman, R., *Pier Soderini and the Ruling Class in Renaissance Florence* (Goldbach: Keip, 2002).

Piqueras Villaldea, M. I., *Carlos V y la Emperatriz Isabel* (Madrid: Actas, 2000).

Pitkin, H. F., *Fortune Is a Woman: Gender and Politics in the Thought of Niccolò Machiavelli* (Berkeley: California University Press, 1984).

Potter, D., 'Politics and faction at the court of Francis I: The Duchesse d'Étampes, Montmorency and the Dauphin Henri', *French History*, 21.2 (2007), 127–46.

Potter, D., *Renaissance France at War* (Woodbridge: Boydell and Brewer, 2008).

Prisco, V., *Eleonora d'Aragona: Pratiche di potere e modelli culturali nell' Italia del Rinascimento* (Rome: Viella, 2022).

Ray, M. *Writing Gender in Women's Letter Collections of the Italian Renaissance* (Toronto: Toronto University Press, 2009).

Reder Gadow, M., 'Isabel de Portugal, Gobernadora De Los Reines de Espana y su proyección de Málaga', *Cuardernos de historia moderna*, 43.2 (2018), 395–423.

Reid, E., 'Female representation and violence in the ceremonial entries of the Italian Wars', *Renaissance Studies*, 36.5 (2022), 750–68.

Reid, E., 'Gendering political relationships in Genoese ceremonial entries', *Sixteenth Century Journal*, 52.1 (2021), 79–110.

Reid, J. A., *King's Sister – Queen of Dissent: Marguerite of Navarre (1492–1549) and Her Evangelical Network*, 2 vols. (Leiden: Brill, 2009).

Réthelyi, O., B. F. Romhányi, E. Spekner, and A. Végh (eds.), *Mary of Hungary: The Queen and Her Court 1521–1531*, trans. A. Harmath, B. F. Romhányi, and G. Trostovszky (Budapest: Budapest History Museum, 2005–6).

Richardson, G., *The Field of Cloth of Gold* (New Haven, CT: Yale University Press, 2013).

Rocke, M., *Forbidden Friendships, Homosexuality and Male Culture in Renaissance Florence* (Oxford: Oxford University Press, 1996).

Rodriguez-Salgado, M. J., 'Charles V and the dynasty', in H. Soly (ed.), *Charles V 1500–1558 and His Time* (Antwerp: Mercartorfonds, 1999), pp. 27–111.

Ross, S. G., *The Birth of Feminism: Woman As Intellect in Renaissance Italy and England* (Cambridge, MA: Harvard University Press, 2009).

Rubio Aragonés, M. J., 'Isabel de Portugal (1503–1539)', *Reinas de Espana, Las Austrias: Siglos XV–XVIII. De Isabel la Cátolica a Marian de Neoburgo* (Madrid: Esfera de los Libros, 2015), pp. 65–108.

Seco Serrano, C., *La Emperatriz Isabel* (Madrid: Real Academia de la Historia, 2006).

Shaw, C., *Isabella d'Este: A Renaissance Princess* (London: Routledge, 2019).

Shaw, C. (ed.), *Italy and the European Powers: The Impact of War* (Leiden: Brill: 2006).

Shaw, C., and M. Mallet, *The Italian Wars 1494–1559: War, State and Society in Early Modern Europe* (London: Routledge, 2014).

Sluga, G., and C. James (eds.), *Women, Diplomacy and Politics since 1500* (London: Routledge, 2016).

Stephenson, B., *The Power and Patronage of Marguerite de Navarre* (Aldershot: Ashgate, 2004).

Swain, E. W., "'My excellent and most singular lord": Marriage in a noble family of fifteenth-century Italy', *Journal of Medieval and Renaissance Studies*, 16 (1986), 171–95.

Syson, L., 'Reading faces: Gian Cristoforo Romano's medal of Isabella d'Este', in C. Mozzarelli, R. Oresko, and L. Venturi (eds.), *La corte di Mantova nell'età di Andrea Mantegna: 1450–1550* (Rome: Bulzoni, 1997), pp. 281–94.

Taylor, F. L. *The Art of War in Italy, 1494–1529* (Cambridge: Cambridge University Press, 1921).

Tomas, N., 'Alfonsina Orsini de' Medici and the "problem" of a female ruler in early sixteenth century Florence', *Renaissance Studies*, 14.1 (2000), 70–90.

Tomas, N., 'Eleonora di Toledo, regency and state formation in Tuscany', in G. Benadusi and J. C. Brown (eds.), *Medici Women: The Making of a Dynasty in Grand Ducal Tuscany* (Toronto: Centre for Reformation and Renaissance Studies, 2015), pp. 59–89.

Tomas, N., *The Medici Women, Gender and Power in Renaissance Florence* (Aldershot: Ashgate, 2003).

Tracy, J. D., *Emperor Charles V, Impresario of War: Campaign Strategy, International Finance, and Domestic Politics* (Cambridge: Cambridge University Press, 2002).

Tylus, J., and G. Milligan (eds.), *The Poetics of Masculinity in Early Modern Italy and Spain* (Toronto: Toronto University Press, 2010).

Villacorta Baños-García, A., *La Emperatriz Isabel* (Madrid: Actas, 2009).

Wilson-Chevalier, K., and E. Pascal (eds.), *Patronnes et mécènes en France à la Renaissance* (Sainte-Etienne: Presses universitaires de Saint-Etienne, 2007).

Winn, C. H., *Approaches to Teaching Marguerite de Navarre's* Heptaméron (Berkeley, CA: Modern Language Association, 2007).

Woodacre, E., L. H. S. Dean, C. Jones, Z. E. Rohr, and R. E. Martin (eds.), *The Routledge History of Monarchy*, 4 vols. (London: Routledge, 2019).

Ylä-Anttila, T., 'Habsburg female regents in the early sixteenth century', unpublished PhD thesis, University of Helsinki (2019).

Acknowledgements

This Element is one of the fruits of a research project on the Italian Wars funded by an Australian Research Council Discovery Grant (DP180102412). We are grateful to the Australian Research Council and our respective universities for supporting our work and acknowledge the importance of our university libraries and the specialist librarians who assisted us in overcoming the problems created by the COVID-19 pandemic in accessing research material. We thank colleagues at the University of Western Australia, Monash University, and the University of Adelaide who assisted us in refining the grant proposal, as well as the advice of the anonymous assessors who reviewed the discovery application. The art historical expertise of our fellow chief investigator, Lisa Mansfield, crucially informed our thinking about the involvement of women in the Italian Wars, as did the insights of Elizabeth Reid, Sarah Bendall, Sally Fisher, Darius Güttner-Sporzyński, Jessica O'Leary, and Emma Nicholls, who met with us regularly over the life of the project and produced sole-authored journal articles and books that explored various aspects of the Wars. Our research has also been enhanced by the expert assistance of Lisa Keane Elliot and Emma Nicholls. We thank the anonymous reviewers of this Element for their expert suggestions and advice.

The pandemic prevented a planned symposium that would have brought a group of internationally renowned scholars to Australia to present their own research and to critique our work in progress. We thank Dagmar Eichberger, Jessica Goethals, Cordula van Whye, James Daybell, and Australian-based scholars John Gagné and Natalie Tomas for their willingness to contribute to the project and deeply regret that the symposium could not take place.

We are grateful to the museums and galleries who kindly agreed to allow us to reproduce images of their holdings. Carolyn thanks the state archives in Mantua and Modena for access to unpublished archival material pertaining to the Gonzaga and Este rulers of Mantua and Ferrara respectively.

Sue thanks Stephen Bowd for sharing early access to a forthcoming publication. She is grateful to Carolyn, from whom she has learned so very much, for her interest in the project from the very beginnings of its life in discussions over lunch at Monash University, and for sharing her deep knowledge and expertise over the course of this work.

The Renaissance

John Henderson

Birkbeck, University of London, and Wolfson College, University of Cambridge

John Henderson is Emeritus Professor of Italian Renaissance History at Birkbeck, University of London, and Emeritus Fellow of Wolfson College, University of Cambridge. His recent publications include *Florence under Siege: Surviving Plague in an Early Modern City* (2019); *Plague and the City*, edited with Lukas Engelmann and Christos Lynteris (2019); and *Representing Infirmity: Diseased Bodies in Renaissance Italy*, edited with Fredrika Jacobs and Jonathan K. Nelson (2021). He is also the author of *Piety and Charity in Late Medieval Florence* (1994); *The Great Pox: The French Disease in Renaissance Europe*, with Jon Arrizabalaga and Roger French (1997); and *The Renaissance Hospital: Healing the Body and Healing the Soul* (2006). Forthcoming publications include a Cambridge Element, *Representing and Experiencing the Great Pox in Renaissance Italy* (2023).

Jonathan K. Nelson

Syracuse University Florence

Jonathan K. Nelson teaches Italian Renaissance art at Syracuse University Florence and is a research associate at the Harvard Kennedy School. His books include *Filippino Lippi* (2004, with Patrizia Zambrano), *Leonardo e la reinvenzione della figura femminile* (2007), *The Patron's Payoff: Conspicuous Commissions in Italian Renaissance Art* (2008, with Richard J. Zeckhauser), and *Filippino Lippi* (2022); and he co-edited *Representing Infirmity: Diseased Bodies in Renaissance Italy* (2021). He co-curated museum exhibitions dedicated to Michelangelo (2002), Botticelli and Filippino (2004), Robert Mapplethorpe (2009), and Marcello Guasti (2019), and two online exhibitions about Bernard Berenson (2012, 2015). Forthcoming publications include a Cambridge Element, *Risks in Renaissance Art: Production, Purchase, Reception* (2023).

Assistant Editor

Sarah McBryde, *Birkbeck, University of London*

Editorial Board

Wendy Heller, *Scheide Professor of Music History, Princeton University*
Giorgio Riello, *Chair of Early Modern Global History, European University Institute, Florence*
Ulinka Rublack, *Professor of Early Modern History, St Johns College, University of Cambridge*
Jane Tylus, *Andrew Downey Orrick Professor of Italian and Professor of Comparative Literature, Yale University*

About the Series

Timely, concise, and authoritative, Elements in the Renaissance showcases cutting-edge scholarship by both new and established academics. Designed to introduce students, researchers, and general readers to key questions in current research, the volumes take multidisciplinary and transnational approaches to explore the conceptual, material, and cultural frameworks that structured the Renaissance experience.

Cambridge Elements ☰

The Renaissance

Printed in the United States
by Baker & Taylor Publisher Services